BUSINESSES DON'T FAIL
They Commit Suicide

How to Survive Success and
Thrive in Good Times and Bad

LARRY MANDELBERG

Businesses Don't Fail, They Commit Suicide
How to Survive Success and Thrive in Good Times and Bad

www.businessesdontfail.com

Date of First Publication: March 21, 2023

Publishing assisted by:
PANDOREN PUBLISHING GROUP
Elk Grove, CA
www.pandoren.com

ISBN 979-8-3019-0649-7

Printed in the United States of America

CONTENTS

ACKNOWLEDGMENTS

This book would not exist without the help of two of my dear friends—Bob Stackhouse, who helped me launch this rocket, and Paul Spector, who helped me land it—and my wife, Nancy, who always helped in ways only a loving, talented, insightful, and caring wife and writer could. In many respects, she was my guide for all the times I felt lost, patient with me when I was buried in my head and unavailable, and my support mechanism when the turmoil I seem to surround myself with became almost too much. Each of these people showed an incredible confidence in my ability to translate my knowledge and experience into a useful book.

To my friends, family, and colleagues: While some of you may be batshit crazy, it takes one to know one, and I don't have the words to express my gratitude and appreciation for your tolerance, support, and patience with me as I've pursued my desire to write this book.

Special thanks go to each beta reader with direct praise for Ariane Cherbuliez, dear friend and coach-extraordinaire, Karl Palachuk, one of the most creative and successful businesspeople I know, and Doug Worth, my friend for life.

To two mentors, the Sacramento Chapter of the California Writers Club, who taught me what professional book writing was, and the Harvest Critique Group, who patiently provided perspectives from mostly nonbusiness backgrounds that helped me think differently, increasing the book's depth and value.

And to everyone whose name escapes me as I transition from writing to promoting. As is often the case with multiyear manuscript journeys, the number of people who have impacted this book is too incalculable to recount. If you touched my life in the past fifty years, you have a hand (or maybe a finger) in the stew that became this book. You've all helped me realize one of my lifelong goals.

With deepest gratitude and respect to you all.

PREFACE

How This Book Came into Being

There are a thousand reasons to blame others for your failure, but none of them will give you success, The only way to succeed in future is by taking responsibility of your present failure.

—Jiten Bhatt[1]

The Question that Drove Me

Ever since I was twelve years old, one question has intrigued me: Why do businesses fail?

I was a child of a business legacy. My father's ancestors came from Russia through Europe landing in Canada in the mid-1800s, where they established our family business selling hides and furs. Failing to adapt to Canada's weather, they moved south to Texas, where the hides and furs business born in Canada transitioned into

---

[1] Bhatt, Jiten. *QuotesLyfe,* https://www.quoteslyfe.com/quote/Take-action-An-inch-of-movement-will-32316

an agricultural scrap-metal and used-equipment business. The heat and humidity eventually drove them north following the path of migrant farmworkers in the late 1800s. The search for home stopped when they reached the Nebraska sand hills and their successful business transitioned once again into agricultural and automotive dealerships, an auto parts store, and machine shop.

Although ours was a small business located in the panhandle of western Nebraska, my father and grandfather had built an interstate reputation for our machine shop work, recognized from Wyoming to Missouri, Texas to North Dakota.

My father didn't particularly like the business we were in even though he was fascinated by it; it was familiar, if not comfortable.

Dad's natural state of being was to worry about something whether he needed to or not. Business is a cruel mistress, always demanding attention, occasionally giving pleasure. Fun and business go together about as well as an accountant doing stand-up comedy. It can happen; it's just not common. This was my introduction to the world of business as the fifth generation of a family-owned business. Doing business was serious.

What Dad really loved was to talk about business. Everywhere we traveled, he talked to any and every local auto parts store owner he could find. A vacation for my father was discussing the business of doing business with business owners regardless of their business. If he couldn't find a business owner, he would go to a local bar and pump the bartender about what it was like to be a bartender. And then he'd ask about the local business climate.

Consumed with his work, my father was full of experiences, questions, and distinctive platitudes—both positive and negative—which he was never shy about sharing.

"Goliath was killed by an assumption."

"No business ever went broke with money in the bank." "Persistence is the most important thing—you can't fail if you never

give up" (one of my personal favorites).

"Giving a customer credit is the most intimate thing you'll ever do."

"What happens if we go to work today and the phone never rings?"

"I'm most worried when everything's running smoothly because I know I'm missing something" (I think this one made us both a bit neurotic).

It was the fall of 1970, a few years before the Arab oil embargo was about to wreak havoc on the US economy. I walked into my father's office where he'd created a cocoon-like comfort zone buried in the bowels of our auto parts store with years of paperwork purposefully piled high enough to create a wall between himself and the world outside.

Louis Mandelberg, Dad, had one of those looks on his face. I knew his head was in there somewhere, back in the past. He was bored and had been reading something from the top of one of the piles near him. Whatever he'd picked up had clearly captured his attention.

> ## Intimacy and Credit
>
> Prior to the 1970s, our auto parts business was 95 percent wholesale, which means we did business with auto repair shops, body shops, car and agricultural dealerships, farmers, and ranchers. When these people needed us, something was broken and they were in a hurry. That meant charge accounts, which allowed us to bring parts and supplies to them, or for them to run into the shop (store) and out quickly with what they needed. Because we were giving them credit for their purchases, we had relationships with them that made their finances our business, to a degree. That was the intimacy he was talking about.

"We went from about three hundred car manufacturers to three in about thirty years," he said. "How did that happen? How can an industry be born, create that many new businesses, then watch most of them go away in such a short time? I can't understand how that's even possible."

His questions got me thinking. My most informed direct business experience was with our family business, which, by that time, had been around for over 120 years. Our location had changed, as had our products and services. We'd adapted to change and survived.

I understood the history of the new car industry even though I really didn't care much about it or why all those car manufacturers had failed, many of them in their early years. As a math geek in grade school and high school, my default thought processes evolved into identifying the facts I had, looking for those I wanted and didn't have, and following a logical path toward a position or belief. What I really wanted to know was what would make any business fail, and I didn't have nearly enough facts.

This way of thinking led me on a journey filled with profound insights. I believed the number of things that could cause businesses to fail was relatively small. I also believed that identifying those things would help me help leaders understand and prepare to avoid whatever was triggering failures before it was too late. Now I needed to figure out what those causes were.

So, why do businesses fail?

My search for the data and the answer began in my teens when I struggled to balance all the distractions of college life against my curiosity. The pull of the search won as my career began in earnest while I worked for auto parts stores and distributors. First in Lincoln, Nebraska, then to Portland, Oregon.

Throughout my time traveling, Dad and I spoke multiple times every week. We were in constant contact, as we had been since I started working with him at age twelve. During one of our conversations while living in Oregon and looking for my next thing, Dad told me he'd always wanted to open a branch in Lake Tahoe, California. We agreed I would go down and check out the business environment while looking for potential auto parts stores whose owners might be willing to sell.

With over twenty auto parts stores around the lake, the economic environment had turned hostile. In addition to the region suffering a devastating drought, interest rates had soared above 20 percent and most of these auto parts stores were on the brink of failure. The Tahoe expedition eventually led to our purchase of an auto parts store about two hundred miles north in Clearlake, California, on February 15, 1980. This was the beginning of my real-world research. I had to close the doors almost six years later. Yes, it seems my failures led to the failure of the business and the inescapable truth that I'd unwittingly committed business suicide. Turns out, I used to be pretty good at doing that, as this wasn't my last time.

In the ensuing thirty-plus years, I've owned ten other businesses representing nine industries. I sold my share of Square Tree Software, my last brick-and-mortar technology company, to my partner on December 31, 1999.

Since 2000, my primary role has been as a consultant, working with leadership teams to evaluate their organizations, share the common problems associated with their stage of maturity,[2] and provide whatever help they need/want to avoid the common pitfalls of change and ensure continuous success.

---

[2] The concept of organizational maturity, the cornerstone of my findings, is covered in chapter 1.

INTRODUCTION

How to Read This Book

I began looking for answers to the elusive "Why do businesses fail?" question in my second decade and found them in my fourth. Realizing the breadth and depth of organizational structures and offerings, I began by defining the attributes of the organizations I wanted to focus on and zeroed in on four:

1. A desire for generational sustainability.
2. More than one layer of management (i.e., organizations where everyone reports to the same person were not my target demographic). This typically results in a minimum of twenty employees.
3. No primary sources of revenue from retail activities. My experience with retail was minimal. While aspects of my findings apply to retail organizations, I have not researched their efficacy in retail environments.
4. Autonomous (i.e., organizations with the ability to make independent decisions based solely on the best interests of the organization). In practice, this means no publicly traded companies or organizations with absentee owners who retain decision-making authority. It also typically results in a maximum of approximately 1,200 employees.

This book chronicles the answer I found after twenty years of primary research with over one hundred companies and 250 executives. It includes my findings, the only three reasons businesses fail, and eight leading nonfinancial indicators of organizational capacity to create profitable growth and sustainability.[3] Together, these indicators become the Mandelberg Business Managers Reality Index (Index).

Completing an Index scorecard survey results in a list of Index indicators ranked by relative strength, unveiling the organization's greatest weaknesses and current level of maturity. The scoring process, an online survey, becomes a psychological commitment because of the implicit need to face the underlying truth of the personal reality of each person who completes one.

Organizational maturity is foundational to my findings and further explained in the first three chapters. The weaker index indicators point leadership to areas that require strengthening. Maximizing each indicator is key to a sustainable, profitable existence while navigating the inevitable changes that occur in good times and bad. I've been successfully using this research to help businesses prepare for and navigate change ever since.

Index validation began with personal interviews of forty-six leaders/owners of companies conducted between May 1, 2003, and January 6, 2005. Their industry segments included legal, marketing, construction and housing, security, accounting, technology, distribution, casinos, nonprofit social benefit organizations, and public sector groups. Between January 6, 2005, and December 2008, I met with approximately sixty additional organizations. In total, over 250 individuals were interviewed.

Each interview included completion of an Index scorecard and review of the results by everyone who completed one, both staff and leadership. Each completed their own scorecard. Roughly half the interviews took thirty to ninety minutes, including explanations and discussion. The balance wanted more details, which took between three and six hours. Due to the slow and often-unrecognized nature of early business failure, evaluating efficacy of the Index can only be

---

[3] My research participants asked a number of questions; most common among them were related to finance, which is addressed in chapter 1. Others frequently asked questions about the age or size of a business, which has no bearing on the likelihood of failure. Every business can fail at any age or size when leadership fails to fulfill their most basic responsibilities—ensuring the 3Ps (Chapter 2) are achieved.

done by leadership and staff within each organization. The results from each completed Index were validated by their respective participants. While a large minority were surprised by their results, *every participant, leadership and staff, felt the Index was accurate.*

This book explains the framework of the Index and how to use it for your organization.

The anecdotes in each chapter are woven with threads of truth spun from personal experiences accumulated through my forty-plus years of business ownership and consulting with clients in each stage of maturity. They highlight one or more aspects of the chapter's content.

As you may suspect, professional ethics and legal confidentiality agreements serve as modesty panels between absolute truth and the details of each anecdote. The anecdotes are designed to create a state of mind that helps you engender empathy for the emotional highs and lows each chapter can evoke. By doing so, my intent is to help cement several truths I've come to believe. I hope you find my storytelling entertaining and effective.

Chapters 1–3 describe the basics of my research. They introduce you to the Index, its eight indicators, the three operational imperatives, the three stages of organizational maturity, and the problems with success. Chapters 4–11 provide insights into each of the indicators, the benefits they provide, and how to create, implement, and maintain them. The last chapter talks about how to get them all implemented.

Proper implementation of the indicators requires strict adherence to the following four principles:

Index principle 1: Must exist in writing.
Index principle 2: Must be clearly and accurately understood.
Index principle 3: Must be shared with the appropriate people at the appropriate times.
Index principle 4: Must be embraced, modeled, and used by leadership and staff.

May this book serve you well.

PART 1

GROWTH AND MATURATION

As this is a business book, I suspect some of you are preoccupied with the absence of a finance chapter and yearning for some numbers. For the concerned or distracted finance-focused readers, here's a bone for you. The number of businesses in the youth stage of maturity is constantly increasing, while the number of businesses in the adolescent and adult stages is constantly decreasing. A steady stream of new organizations launches every day.

Most of them start with inexperienced leadership taking their first entrepreneurial steps. Because there are more of these businesses than adolescent or mature businesses, there are more opportunities for failure and more failures.

This will be true for the foreseeable future, certainly until America stops fostering entrepreneurship and innovation, which I don't see happening in my lifetime. Even during periods of natural disasters such as the COVID-19 pandemic of 2020, new opportunities arise just as stability tends to become less certain. Entrepreneurship and the ability to achieve personal goals are fundamental aspects of the American dream. It's in our DNA, something that can't be extracted or suppressed regardless of the political or economic climate.

CHAPTER 1

A Murder Mystery... or Was It Suicide?

It ain't what you don't know that gets you into trouble. It's what you know for sure that just ain't so.

—Samuel Clemens[4]

If you struggle with the idea of a business committing suicide, how do you explain what happens when a business fails? Clearly, a business can be intentionally driven to failure, yet the thought of such an effort seems foolish and not in keeping with the general intent of a business.

How then does a business fail? If failure is not self-inflicted, how do we determine the cause? Regardless of the environment or circumstances around its failure, when a well-conceived business fails, something has gone wrong.

I believe responsibility for organizational success belongs exclusively to leadership. These are the people with authority to make any decision they deem necessary for the health and well-being of their organizations. It is also their responsibility to ensure the organization survives, if not

---

[4] Clemens, Samuel. "Mark Twain > Quotes > Quotable Quote," *Goodreads.* Goodreads Inc. https://www.goodreads.com/quotes/7588008-it-ain-t-what-you-don-t-know-that-gets-you-into.

thrives. Therefore, failure, whether unintended or deliberate, is a failure of leadership. As a failure of leadership, it becomes self-inflicted.

Hence, self-inflicted failure is business suicide.

While there are many ways to interpret the meaning of business suicide, this book is an exploration of how to avoid it and build a successful, thriving business.

Sidecar Coffee

It was five thirty in the morning and still dark out. I didn't realize Sidecar Coffee wasn't open until I pulled into their empty parking lot.

Maybe they're closed on Mondays. I'm sure I've been here on a Monday before...haven't I?

Got out of my car and walked through drizzling rain up to the front door looking for their hours or something that said they were closed on Mondays.

But no.

What I saw was a building with coffee-brewing equipment, trash, pieces of shelving, and display cases, all broken and strewn haphazardly across the hollow interior of a once-thriving coffee shop. And there I stood. Cold. Wet. Dazed.

Gone. When? Why? But...crap, where am I going to get...

Not really a big deal, certainly not a problem with a Starbucks on every corner. It wasn't that I couldn't get my espresso; it was that

---

A Well-conceived Business

1. It offers one or more products and/or services desired by an existing market.

2. It offers its product(s) and/or service(s) for a cost that allows them to be sold/exchanged at an affordable price to the customer.

3. It exists to fulfill a need that has sufficient market demand and market capacity to purchase its products and/or services.

4. It offers and produces/delivers its product(s) and/or service(s) at a cost that allows for sufficient profits/funding to cover the costs of maintenance, operations, new product/service development, growth and, in the case of for-profit organizations, a return on investment.

---

my comfort zone had been invaded and all that was left were the broken remnants of a business I still felt very connected to.

What happened to Michael? I hope he's okay. Why didn't he say anything? Maybe I could have helped.

I was having some trouble absorbing the reality staring me in the face—my friend, entrepreneur, and favorite barista was gone…

Why Do Businesses Fail?

The Sidecar Coffee story is about business failure with no readily apparent reason. Business failures have always been far too common for me even when environmental factors like the Great Recession[5] that began in December 2007 and the COVID-19 pandemic of 2020 are considered. While leaders of failed businesses I've spoken with have reasons, those reasons usually sounded more like excuses, as if the leaders never really understood what happened and why their businesses failed.

The COVID-19 Factor

From Barron's "The Striking Price" column on December 28, 2020, titled *Placing a Bullish Bet on Disney Before Earnings.*

Walt Disney's strategic pivot in 2020—one of the worst years imaginable for a theme-park operator—is a case study of how effective leaders are often a company's most important asset.

Executive abilities are never carried on a corporate balance sheet or given some tangible valuation, but Disney executives are proof of just how much a good team can accomplish even under dramatic pressures that seem to threaten the economic essence of their company (italic emphasis added by Mandelberg).

When investors were determined to see nothing but trouble for Disney as the COVID-19 pandemic threatened earnings by shuttering theme parks, the company's leaders developed a streaming-content strategy that has seemingly changed the company's fortunes on Wall Street.

Disney stock, which was largely written off as a casualty of the COVID-19 pandemic, has since become one of the great success stories of a difficult year. Shares are trading near a fifty-two-week high, and investors are excited about the future, especially as the pandemic seems poised to end in 2021 thanks to the vaccine rollout.

---

5 History.com Editors. "Great Recession," *History*, A&E Television Networks LLC, 11 October 2019, https://www.history.com/topics/21st-century/recession.

The question arose for me when my father's curiosity led him to ask me how hundreds of automobile manufacturers came into being between the late 1800s and 1908 only to see most fail over the next three decades with Ford, General Motors (GM), and Chrysler dominating the market. Having no idea how to answer him and unfamiliar with formal research practices, my curiosity had been kindled.

With no internet, efforts to find answers began with conversations with other business leaders I was exposed to through my activities at school, traveling with my family, and at our auto parts store. My informal research began in the summer of 1975 between high school and college with a focus on start-ups.

Start-ups were easy to find and appeared to do a lot of failing. The most frequent comment I heard from people who had reason to know something about them was, start-ups usually failed in the first three years, and any that survived would probably last a lot longer.

Taking their comments as factual, I concluded start-ups must suffer some form of false belief caused by inexperience and lack of maturity, much like teenagers—certain they know everything there is to know, unaware of risks, and routinely getting into trouble. Being immature and inexperienced made no sense to me for two reasons.

First, starting a new business requires money. Whether a

> ### The Auto Parts Business
>
> New automobile manufacturers started appearing in the US in 1893. Thirty American manufacturers produced 2,500 motor vehicles in 1899, and some 485 companies entered the business in the next decade. The number of active automobile manufacturers dropped from 253 in 1908 to only 44 in 1929, with about 80 percent of the industry's output accounted for by Ford, General Motors, and Chrysler, formed from Maxwell in 1925 by Walter P. Chrysler.[6] (A loss of 471 new car manufacturers, 91.5 percent, in a thirty-year period.)

---

[6] Bicycle mechanics J. Frank and Charles Duryea of Springfield, Massachusetts, had designed the first successful American gasoline automobile in 1893, then won the first American car race in 1895, and went on to make the first sale of an American-made gasoline car the next year. History.com Editors. "Automobile History," *History*, A&E Television Networks LLC, 21 August 2018, https://www.history.com/topics/inventions/automobiles.

self-funded entrepreneur or financed by third parties, few are willing to invest in a start-up if they believe it's likely to fail in three years. If failing in their first three years was accurate, investors would figure out what was causing failure and how to avoid it.

Second, many start-ups were successful the moment they launched. They made money, grew, and prospered for years and years. My research indicated their success wasn't related to planning or any lack thereof. There had to be something different about the start-ups that became successful and avoided the three-year failure scenario. This second reason turned out to be the key to finding my answer.

Experience is the teacher of all things. (Julius Caesar)[7]

The successful businesses in my initial research had leadership teams with prior relevant experience. I'm not saying every business with experienced leadership succeeded. I am saying those who succeeded had support and guidance from people who'd been through the grind in one way or another and didn't need to do much learning on the fly.

Additionally, documenting details of businesses that eventually failed helped me recognize their failures had nothing to do with their age. Although start-up failures were often connected to lack of leadership team experience, the reasons for success and failure were much more complicated.

A speaker at the 2007 annual conference of the Institute of Management Consultants—USA, Michael Mann, shared a wonderful

> ## What Is a Start-Up?
>
> For the purposes of this book, I define a start-up as a new organization created by a handful of people with few, if any, customers, products, or services. They tend to be funded by the founder, their friends and family, and operate informally. While information in this book has been used and proven valuable to several start-ups, it is not written with them in mind. See the introduction for more details.

---

[7] Caesar, Gaius Julius. "Gaius Julius Caesar > Quotes > Quotable Quote," *Goodreads.* https://www.goodreads.com/quotes/308892-experience-is-the-teacher-of-all-things.

story about Sam Walton, founder of Walmart. It brings the concept of experience and how it relates to maturity vs. age into sharp relief.

Sam Walton was known for avoiding interviews and publicity. Through a series of unplanned events, a high school girl found herself in Sam's office interviewing him for a school project.

"Mr. Walton, you've become one of the most successful businessmen in the world. To what do you owe all your success?" asked the student.

"Good decisions," Walton answered without hesitation.

Somewhat surprised by his swift and succinct response, the student paused to gather herself, took a deep breath, and asked, "Mr. Walton, how did you learn how to make good decisions?"

Again, Walton barely took a breath before replying, "Experience."

The girl was frustrated and struggled to hide her dismay. It was clear her interview was not going the way she had expected. "Mr. Walton, how did you get *your* experience?"

"Bad decisions," he said after a brief and powerful pause.

Thus endeth the interview.

Experiences are the bricks that pave the road to maturity. Maturity is what you acquire as you make the journey and grows with each new experience. Organizational maturity encompasses both leadership and staff. My research led to the natural segmentation of maturity into three stages:

- Youth: minimal organizational experience
- Adolescence: narrowly focused depth of organizational experience
- Adulthood: broad and deep organizational experience

Each stage of maturity correlates to the depth and breadth of accumulated leadership and staff experience. Understanding the relationship between experience and maturity will help leaders apply the concepts in this book and minimize the bad decisions that lead to self-destructive mistakes.

It's Not Bad Luck, It's Bad Leadership

One of my first analytic efforts was to inventory potential triggers of business failure and look for ways to avoid them. Part of the process involved finding businesses that were suffering, exploring the context and underlying factors of their problems with their owners and managers, and documenting them. Zeroing in on the problems and underlying factors became an interesting exercise.

Most of the businesspeople I spoke with thought they knew exactly what their problems were, which was a problem in and of itself. As a financially disinterested observer, it was easier for me to see their perceived problems were actually symptoms. Their inability to recognize the underlying problems behind the symptoms (what I call root problems) was part of why these businesses were in distress. In effect, treating symptoms ignores problems, and treatment efforts will likely be fruitless.

Once I recognized the tendency to focus on symptoms as root problems, I began looking for indicators that would consistently and accurately predict potential business failure.

Symptom	Root Problem
Dramatic loss of revenue due to external forces (i.e., it wasn't our fault).	Dependence on limited, interrelated revenue sources.[8]
Receivables eating up available cash and turning sales staff into debt collectors.	Sales and collection systems are not aligned with customer ecosystems or internal operational needs.
Internal silos keep departments and staff from talking and working with each other.	Failure to demonstrate how individual and organizational success depends on the coordinated efforts of many.

---

[8] Many small businesses, including retail and restaurants, were able to survive the COVID-19 economic crises of 2020–21 due to diverse and creative approaches to delivering value to their customer base and finding new markets to serve.

One or more managers routinely losing staff and ignoring the rules.	Poor recruiting, onboarding, training, and/or management of managers.
Operations are a bureaucratic nightmare where nothing gets done.	Authorities and responsibilities are out of balance.

While these are generic examples, they expose the urgent and emotional aspects of symptoms. It becomes easier to see how the focus of management can be captured by symptoms while root problems tend to remain hidden or overlooked.

"…lack of funds is a lagging financial indicator and can never be the reason a business fails."

Virtually everyone I spoke with included money as part of why their organization failed, as if more cash or credit would have given them time to solve their problems. Most of the time, in my experience, the impact of having more money is more money wasted coupled with delayed failure. Unfortunately, for those looking for excuses, lack of funds is a lagging financial indicator and can never be the reason a business fails.

All financial indicators are objective measures of historic reality and can't expose problems until they're revealed in a reporting mechanism. By the time they are identified, it's likely the harm has been done.

"While financial problems are never the cause of failure, they are critically important as lagging indicators of bad decisions—"

When a business starts having problems with cash, it's an important symptom of something wrong. What the lack of cash doesn't tell you is what that something is. That's where leadership needs to be on its toes. While financial problems are never the cause of failure, they are critically important as lagging indicators of bad decisions—decisions that are either poorly thought-out, poorly executed, or in pursuit of inappropriate objectives.

As I began writing this book, a colleague noticed that there was no chapter on finance.

"How can you write a business book without a chapter on finance?" he asked.

I explained that my research led me to some interesting realities about money and finance. It's not the lack of money that causes problems. Most often, it's the business's inability to manage its financial resources.

At this point, I had accumulated some good information and identified several important business failure facts (BFFs 😖 😳 😌):

- Symptoms are often identified and treated as root problems.
- Finance is a lagging indicator of existing problems, aka a symptom, never the root cause.
- Start-ups that survive have access to experienced leadership.

These findings became the seeds of the Mandelberg Business Managers Reality Index (the Index), the tool I developed to measure the capacity of an organization to create sustainable, profitable growth using leading nonfinancial indicators, aka to *thrive and survive*.

The Common Denominator

The reason for chasing all this data was to find leading indicators that would help businesses and their leadership teams avoid unintentional, unnecessary, and premature failure. I searched for those indicators through nine years of education, running multiple businesses, and twenty years of talking to businesspeople. After combining that research with 150+ years of family business knowledge and experience, I eventually came to understand a simple truth that was the key to developing the Index.

A successful and well-managed business doesn't spontaneously start having problems. Problems begin when change happens.

Change was the common denominator in every business failure I'd researched, yet I still didn't have the answer. I did have a lot of questions.

> *What aspects of change were harmful enough to cause a business to fail?*

> *If change is inevitable and the underlying cause of failure, how can a business protect itself in a constantly changing world?*

> *How can a business create the durability and resilience to adapt to constant change?*

> *What does a business need to do with unwavering consistency to thrive despite the changes happening around it?*

When anything in the business environment changes, whether internally or externally, the business will be impacted. It could be a new competitor or service that makes your offerings less valuable. It could be internal departments adjusting to meet client demands and creating confusion for the customer about whom to contact when help is needed. Change often creates unexpected problems with no instructions on how to handle them. When leadership doesn't have the experience to deal with those problems, they can make mistakes that accumulate and eventually harm the business.

It's not just the sense of doing something wrong; it's the sense of not knowing what to do and being forced to rely on experiences that have limited relevance to the immediate problem. All too often, solutions that worked under different circumstances can be toxic when used to solve current problems. When the wrong solution is implemented, the degree to which the business is impacted can vary, but there is always an impact. When the impact is small, it can go unnoticed or get lost in the day-to-day activities of the business. When the impact is substantial, it can create serious issues.

Key Points

Businesses have been starting and suffering the destructive effects of change ever since mankind grasped the idea that goods and services can be exchanged for mutual benefit. The ability to anticipate and smooth the disruptions of constant change is a trademark of good leadership.

A successful and well-managed business doesn't spontaneously start having problems. Problems begin when change happens.

Mistaking symptoms as problems is one of several destructive behaviors that underlay leaderships' inability to deal with change efficaciously.

There are three stages of organizational maturity, which encompasses both leadership and staff:

- *Youth*: minimal organizational experience
- *Adolescence*: narrowly focused depth of organizational experience
- *Adulthood*: broad and deep organizational experience

Each stage of maturity correlates to the depth and breadth of accumulated leadership and staff experience.

This concept of maturity is foundational to all the information in this book.

CHAPTER 2

Operational Imperatives of Leadership, aka The 3 Ps

Can a business have a mind, a sub-conscious, a knack for predicting the future, reflexes faster than the speed of thought? Can a business have a spirit? Can a business have a soul? Can a business be alive?

—SAP television ad campaign[9]

How a Business Commits Suicide

Each stage of maturity has an operational imperative for healthy, sustainable growth to be realized. Every business failure is a human failure attributable to the failure of leadership to achieve an operational imperative.

Stage of Maturity	Operational Imperative (3Ps)
Youth	Clarity of Purpose
Adolescence	Consistency of Performance
Adulthood	Engagement[10] of People

---

[9] From an SAP (sap.com) television ad campaign, summer 2016.

[10] "A workplace method designed to improve an employee's feelings and emotional attachment to the company, their job duties, position within the company, their fellow employees, and the company culture." "What Is the Definition of Employee Engagement?" Retrieved February 11, 2019. https://www.bamboohr.com/hr-glossary/employee-engagement-in-hr.

Organizations at the youth stage fail due to insufficient clarity of *purpose*, those at the adolescent stage fail due to inconsistent *performance*, and adult stage entities fail due to their inability to effectively engage *people*. I call them the three Ps (3Ps).

Achieving each of the 3Ps at their appropriate stages of your business' maturity is the most direct and assured path to profitable sustainability. Failure to achieve them leads to the only truly destructive problems at the heart of any business' demise. Everything else from poor financial management to bad employees to dishonest customers, even natural disasters such as the COVID-19 pandemic, can be neutralized by achieving and maintaining the 3Ps.

Over the years, we've all had the unfortunate experience of witnessing dozens of business failures. I've even had a few of my own. My sense of loss has been consistent though the intensity varied based on the degree of personal involvement.

Each time, whether mine or not, I go through the mental exercise of asking "Why?" "What happened?" "Could I have done something?" and an assortment of related questions to help me feel better about my loss. I say my loss because there's usually a personal connection, whether it's one of the many businesses in my neighborhood I routinely drive past or a corporate giant like Woolworths. Too often my routines are disrupted when a local business, such as Sidecar Coffee, isn't there anymore.

As I began developing my theory on business failure and gaining clarity about the reasons, the emotions I felt mirrored what I felt when someone died. When a business fails, its stakeholders experience a sense of loss. From employees to customers, something they knew, cared about, and often depended on is gone—an emotional experience similar to a death or suicide.

The good news about business failure is that well-conceived businesses don't fail due to external forces. They failed because leadership didn't ensure the operational imperatives were achieved and sustained over time and through periods of change.

Diving deeper into why the imperatives hadn't been achieved, I found surprising answers:

- Leadership *didn't know* they needed to achieve them.
- Leadership *didn't care* about achieving them.
- Leadership *didn't know how* to achieve them.
- Leadership *forgot* to sustain them.

Youth and the First P
Clarity of Purpose

While profits or revenues are critical to maintaining operations and delivering value, regardless of organizational structure, they are an insufficient indicator of success. The concept that a business exists to make money is the conventional viewpoint. In my experience, profit without purpose is pointless and unsustainable.

> *"…profit without purpose is pointless and unsustainable."*

Purpose is about providing value and delivering it. An organization without it is a rudderless ship floating in a sea of endless opportunities and no destination. Where are we going, and why are we headed there? Without purpose, profits are typically short-lived. As stated in chapter 1, organizations at the youth stage with minimal organizational experience fail primarily due to insufficient clarity of purpose.

Clarity of purpose is measured with the Index based on the status of three indicators:

1. The cultural framework: values statements
2. What you want your business to become: vision statement
3. The value your business delivers: mission statement

Chapter 4—The Cultural Framework: Values

There are many ways to achieve a vision and fulfill a mission, behavioral options that lie well within the bounds of legal activity. Values provide boundaries for what an organization will or won't do in pursuit of its vision and mission. They establish a behavioral framework for how employees will act under stress or difficult circumstances and serve as the foundation for corporate culture.

The most effective way to proactively design a culture is through values statements. Too many organizations create them for the wrong reasons and fail to educate or enforce them. Values statements provide answers to some of the most difficult decisions while reinforcing the mission and vision. Together, they create clarity of purpose and form a solid foundation for success.

Chapter 5—What You Want Your Business to Become: Vision Statement

When an organization clearly communicates its long-term goals, each employee can connect with something bigger than themselves. These goals and objectives provide the reasons staff work late and miss dinner or their children's activities. Long-term goals are achieved by motivated people proud of what they're achieving.

The most effective way to communicate this aspect of purpose is with a thoughtfully crafted vision statement. It should be the first and most prominent *internally-facing* message your staff and prospective candidates should see and hear, why they would want to join you and your team on your journey to achieve the vision. The ability to emotionally connect the work your organization is doing with a bigger purpose is a profound component of sustainability.

Chapter 6—The Value Your Business Delivers: Mission Statement

When an organization is clear about the value it delivers, whom it delivers to, and how it is delivered, operational details tend to fall into place. Clarity of value creates guidelines for structure, marketing, sales, and support. It also ensures the organization focuses on selling the right products and services to the right markets and avoids wasting time and money trying to sell to the wrong markets.

The most effective way to communicate this aspect of purpose is with a well-crafted mission statement. It should be the first and most prominent *customer-facing* message your prospects see and hear, why they should do business with you. Pundits may have given up on the value of mission and vision statements. Part of that is due to leaderships' struggle to create statements that can be believed and embraced. Mission statements do have value when used correctly. The ability to communicate your value clearly and concisely to your market becomes a fundamental component of sustainability.

Adolescence and the Second P
Consistency of Performance

Cost and quality are the two most manageable attributes of product and service delivery. As the saying goes, you can have it cheap or you can have it good, but you can't have it good and cheap. While there is truth to that saying, it doesn't identify the secret to success with respect to delivery, aka performance.

When it comes to delivering products and services, consistent levels of performance outweigh all other aspects of the end-user experience. Buyers expect to get what they pay for. An organization that cannot consistently fulfill the expectations of its customers is undependable. Performance is about setting expectations and delivering on them. Without consistent performance, customers are short-lived. As stated in chapter 1, organizations at the adolescent stage with narrowly focused depth of organizational experience fail primarily due to inconsistent performance.

Consistency of performance is measured with the Index by the status of three indicators:

4. How your organization delivers on its mission: business plan
5. How the business finds and creates demand for products and services: marketing plans
6. What each employee is responsible for: goals and responsibilities

Chapter 7—Strategies and Tactics: Business Plan

When an organization is clear about the way it conducts its business, ambiguity is replaced by clarity. Operational guidelines such as target markets, ideal clients, and policies and procedures are tools that help employees do their job and customers conduct business with the company. Customers know what to expect, and expectations are fulfilled.

I've found the most effective way to communicate these aspects of performance to staff is with a business plan. Often referred to as a road map, the business plan connects the operations of the business with the expectations of its customers and leadership. The ability to map out the activities of your organization is one of the fundamental components of success.

Chapter 8—Finding Customers: Marketing Plans

When an organization communicates to the markets it's designed to serve and the benefits it delivers, prospective buyers develop an awareness of the company and the value they can receive from engaging with it. A connection evolves between the consumer and provider when need is served. That connection is the basis for long-term relationships and mutual benefit.

The most effective way to ensure the right message is being timely delivered to the right markets is by developing marketing plans. Marketing plans create insight into the value of the company's products and services along with the level of demand for them. The ability to understand and act on these needs is another fundamental component of success.

Chapter 9—Who Empties the Trash: Goals and Responsibilities

Having a business plan to provide direction and marketing plans to provide messaging is not enough to achieve success. The individuals that make up the organization need to understand who is responsible for each aspect of these two functions. This is frequently referred to as division of labor. Everyone in the organization must understand their roles and have the ability to perform them.

> *"When leadership fails to provide the proper framework for staff, peak performance can be elusive, and the best efforts of good people are often wasted."*

Commonly referred to as job descriptions, their value diminishes as they become stale while the jobs they're defining evolve. The most valuable asset any business has is its employees. When leadership fails to provide the proper framework for staff, peak performance can be elusive, and the best efforts of good people are often wasted.

Adulthood and the Third P
Engagement of People

A business is a reflection of the people who work in it. Staff are closest to the organization's clients, touch all areas of client activity, and are the first to see problems as they begin to develop. The tone of each customer experience is defined by their interactions with staff. Every aspect of every organization is impacted by the people working in it.

Doing business with an organization is always enhanced or diminished by the experience the customer has with its employees—there's no room for ambivalence. When staff are inspired and engaged, working with a company and working for a company are joyful experiences. As stated in chapter 1, organizations at the adult stage with broad and deep organizational experience fail primarily due to their inability to effectively engage people.

Engagement of people is measured with the Index by the status of two indicators:

7. How work flows through the organization: systems and structure
8. How information is kept current and shared: communication plans

Chapter 10—How Work Flows through the Business: Systems and Structure

The desire to do something productive is a normal aspect of human nature. Understanding the way things work within an organization accomplishes two goals: First, it gives staff the ability to recognize the role they play in the creation and delivery of value to each client. Second, it gives staff the opportunity to identify new and better ways of doing so.

One of the most potent ways to develop these skills is by documenting the systems and structure that define how the organization operates. When employees connect their efforts to the value the company delivers, they become more engaged and take greater pride in their work. Documenting the processes of an organization is one of the structural components of success.

The Problem with Job Descriptions

The traditional label for goals and responsibilities is job description. I've found describing a job is more akin to programming tasks into a non-AI computer. The key to what's behind every member of any organization lives within the goals they are expected to achieve and the responsibilities they are expected to fulfill. That's a lot more than a job description.

A favorite example of this relates to routine maintenance. Do you want someone to empty the trash every day (a task)? Or keep the office clean (a goal)? Do you want an office manager to order supplies (a task) or ensure staff have the resources to do their jobs effectively (a goal)?

It sounds simple, and it can be if you adjust your way of thinking a bit. This concept—goals and responsibilities—applies to every job from the CEO/president to receptionist and all positions in between.

Chapter 11—Information Sharing: Communication Plans

Curiosity is a normal and healthy aspect of human nature. Timely access to relevant information eliminates fear, frustration, and uncertainty. The ability to get answers to questions creates confidence and eliminates resistance to action. Being a source of information creates a sense of value and contribution.

Knowing where to get information is just as important as knowing when and how to share it when need arises. One of the most effective ways to ensure information is available to the right people at the right time is with a robust communications plan. Developing a robust communications plan is one of the structural components of success.

*****

Each of the eight Index indicators represents a structural component of your business. In chapter 1, I describe how experiences are the bricks that pave the road to maturity. Like experiences, these indicators help create the structural integrity of profitable sustainability.

A building is built in planned, sequential steps starting with the foundation, then the framing, exterior, and finally, the interior. So, too, does profitable business sustainability require planned, sequential steps to build structural integrity by successfully implementing each indicator of the Index in the proper order based on its stage of maturity.

Many businesses have several Index indicators already in place. Most have gaps that need to be filled in. As you go through this book, each indicator is explained along with insights on how to create, implement, and maintain them.

"each of the eight index indicators represents a structural component of your business."

As indicators of sustainability, each has a substantive role in the tactical operations of every organization. Leadership teams that care about the long-term survival of their organizations should create and implement all eight indicators. The overhead to put each in place is not trivial and should be undertaken with an earnest sense of value and commitment. The process of creation for one can be similar for others (e.g., chapter 9, "Who Empties the Trash: Goals and Responsibilities" in adolescence, and chapter 10, "How Work Flows through the Business: Systems and Structure" in adulthood).

I encourage you to focus on one Index indicator at a time and avoid efforts to save time or cut corners by working on any of the three phases: creation, implementation, or maintenance for multiple indicators simultaneously. I caution you to work on the indicators within your stage of maturity in the order they are presented in the Index. If you have indicators already in place, such as business or marketing plans, revisit and/or revise them at the appropriate time as your organization progresses through the Arc of Success (chapter 3) and matures.

Lack of Index Indicator Standards

There is no universally accepted definition of what a mission statement is. In practice, I've found substantial inconsistencies with what people believe vision, mission, and purpose statements are and how they differ.

So, too, are there substantial differences among senior-most experts as to what belongs in a business or marketing plan. And communications plans are so pervasive throughout so many industries serving so many purposes, consensus around a single standard seems impossible.

The absence of commonly accepted definitions or standards results in the form and function of each indicator being subject to interpretation. Most people have been exposed to each indicator, which has impacted both their understanding and attitude toward them and their value to an organization.

Therefore, the accuracy and value of the Index are dependent on a specific understanding of each indicator as defined in chapters 4–11.

Pam's Anecdote
One Leader's Journey of Success

The following interview reflects one special entrepreneur's successful journey through each stage of maturity from start-up to retirement, an example of the ups and downs of change.

*****

Professor: "I'd like to thank our audience for suffering the wind and icy conditions outside to hear today's speaker, Pamela Jonas. Those of you interested in what it means to be a financially successful entrepreneur are going to enjoy our guest today. As one of our hometown success stories, Pam is the retired founder and former CEO of an energy company she started almost forty years ago. Her firm began as a two-person start-up and grew into a publicly traded, multibillion-dollar, multinational solar company. And with that, let me start by asking you, Pam. Tell us about some of the most memorable experiences you had building and leading Sustainable Energy Solutions."

Pam: "First, Professor, thank you for the opportunity to speak with UC Boulder's next crop of engineering leaders and entrepreneurs. You've asked a great question. It's something I've spent a lot of time thinking about since I retired last year, and there are two that really stand out for me.

"You might think the first one was when we started, which was exciting and fun, but it wasn't the most memorable. I'd been dreaming of starting my company for years, and when it finally happened, it wasn't really anything special for me, it was more of a feeling that I didn't have to wait any longer. Now it was time to get moving on my dream, which we did.

"The first experience that stood out for me was about a year after we were first featured in Entrepreneurship, the online community for start-ups and entrepreneurs. Clearly, the right people found out about us, and we took off like a rocket after that. It felt like somebody had fired a starter pistol at a track race and overnight we were moving at eighty miles an hour. Just trying to keep up with demand was almost impossible, and we hadn't learned how to say no yet. "Everything everybody wanted" was our motto at the time, and more was always better. We never even thought about the ramifications or saw the wall we were about to run into.

"By the time we hit the wall, we'd grown to a twenty-eight-person company, and everybody was doing everything. Most of us were engineers, and we didn't really need any sales or marketing skills. We just needed to make sure we filled orders. The thing none of us saw was our lack of knowledge and inexperience with matters of finance. One day the bank called and told me we had no money in the checking account. They knew we had a payroll to make in a few days, and I was devastated.

"I knew something had to change. What I didn't know was what we were doing wrong or how we needed to change. I called friends and family looking for help, but the hole we'd dug was just too big for them to help us. Eventually, I had to go to the bank and tell them the truth. I had no money and no idea where to get it. That was a very memorable and painful experience."

Professor: "Doesn't sound very pleasant to me, nor comfortable. So what did you do?"

Pam: "The bank was great. They knew exactly what had been happening and had been expecting us to run out of money, so it was no surprise to them. They had a consultant they worked with who helped companies with this same problem. The way he described it was that it was time for us to change our focus from 'more is better' to 'better is more.' Took me a while for that to sink in, but when it did, it made a lot of sense. Then I had to get my team on board. It felt like the consultant was telling us to make a U-turn with an oil tanker barreling east at full speed and instantly head west.

"We'd been selling anything to anyone as long as they had money. The problem was, we were dealing with hypergrowth that we'd never planned. We just started spending money to keep up without having any operational controls in place. We had no clear job descriptions, so we had a lot of duplication of effort. We had no systems or processes in place, so we were also wasting a lot of time doing things inefficiently in one area, while another group was doing the same thing very efficiently, but nobody knew.

"We were investing enormous amounts of energy trying to sell and service small, one-off customers who consumed far too much time and money for the returns we were getting. There was no ability to leverage anything because every customer was different. Once we were able to figure out how much it was costing us to serve all those unique individual clients, we realized we had to get very clear about what we were going to be selling and whom we were going to be selling to.

"Perhaps the worst thing was that our quality started to slip. Things began falling through the cracks because the pressure on staff caused by our lack of systems and inability to leverage what we were doing across a broad spectrum of customers was debilitating. No wonder things were falling through the cracks. It felt like we were killing ourselves. I like to say we were committing business suicide without ever knowing it. That's when I said, 'No more, something has to change.'

"What the consultant meant when he said we needed to move from 'more is better' to 'better is more' was beginning to come into focus for me. We put in controls, systems, guidelines, all the administrative overhead, things a start-up never seems to have the time to develop—the structure that was critical for ensuring we were effective, efficient, and prepared for whatever was in front of us. Suddenly it felt like we were running a brand-new business, and it was fun again.

"We were lucky we didn't lose the business. If it hadn't been for some insightful and trusting people at the bank, we would never have recovered."

Professor: "Sounds pretty awful, Pam. I'm a little nervous to ask about the other experience!"

Pam: "The good news is, it wasn't as frightening, or at least it doesn't sound that way. But it was a very different problem we'd grown into.

"Once we got a handle on the business, it felt like we were on top of the world. Everything an entrepreneur could dream of.

International recognition, covers of the top business publications, incredible growth, and the cash was just flooding in. Thank goodness we'd put very good financial controls in place or we would have blown it all.

"It wasn't long after that when our investors started asking about exit strategies… It was time to go public."

Professor: "That must have made you feel very proud after all you and your team had been through."

Pam: "It did, of course, but that's not what was memorable. Going public is a familiar story to many, something many truly successful businesses achieve. The thing that I remember was not a success, but our next failure, or as I prefer to think of it, our next 'most valuable lesson.'

"We'd built a strong and talented leadership team, and obviously, we were all working very well together. We weren't going to let ourselves be blindsided like we were before. As someone once said, 'It's not what you don't know that gets you in trouble, it's what you know for sure that just ain't so.' That's what happened to us."

Professor: "What was the problem, Pam, and how did it come to your attention?"

Pam: "It was something I never would have expected, which, of course, is exactly how businesses and leadership teams like ours get into trouble. When a business experiences something for the first time, you just don't know what to look for, so you never recognize a problem before it becomes painful. When it does, then you have to go into damage-control mode and start repairs. That's what happened to us."

Professor: "How so?"

Pam: "The first sign of the problem was when I noticed our employment costs trending up, well beyond the ratio we'd budgeted. It took our HR department some time to figure it out because the impact was spread over a number of different areas. We'd grown to almost three thousand people by then, and what I'd found and hadn't yet realized was that our staff was disengaged. I know *engagement* is one of those popular buzzwords in the HR community. I'd heard of it and never really understood what employee engagement meant.

"The impact was widespread. First, we were losing some of our best and most talented people. They were just quitting for no particular reason we could identify. Second, people stopped looking for ways to be innovative, to do things better, more efficiently. As we'd grown, our systems and structure had remained static.

"What once was helpful had quickly become harmful. Staff were doing things because that's how they'd always been done. Nobody was asking if any of our systems or processes needed to be revised. Our managers had grown comfortable in their roles. They were reluctant to accept, much less listen, to any talk about change. The smart people were tired of trying to change those things they knew could be done better.

"What was worse, managers and some of my senior staff had become so protective of their turf they were delegating responsibility to others without giving them the authority to be successful with their delegated tasks. We'd become a classic bureaucracy."

Professor: "That's fascinating, Pam, and I suspect this happens to a lot of large, successful companies."

Pam: "Yes. Once again, we almost killed ourselves, and as you might imagine, I was pretty upset. I remember yelling at my husband one night, 'When am I going to stop getting hit by new things? When is this going to start getting easier?' That's when he told me that change is constant, and I knew what he meant. If things ever stopped changing, we were going to be dead.

"So we reached out as a leadership team to a consultant who had dealt with this before and had helped one of his clients get through it. We changed much of the way we operated. We reorganized and began doing things that helped our staff understand how their efforts fit into the bigger picture and contributed in a material, meaningful way to our success.

"This is a much longer story than we have time for here. We did survive, obviously, and began to grow again. Eventually, we got to where we are now, and I finally felt like the company I'd given birth to was mature enough to go out into the world on its own and thrive without me."

Key Points

Ch 1	Operational Imperatives	Clarity of purpose	Consistency of performance	Engagement of people
Ch 2	Stage of Maturity	Youth	Adolescence	Adulthood
Ch 2	Why leaders fail to achieve the 3 P's	They didn't know they needed to do them.	They didn't know how to do them.	They forgot they needed to do them.

With people, age and maturity are not interdependent or linked. Having lived many years does not mean an adult is mature. I know many immature adults. Having lived a few years does not preclude a child from behaving maturely—I also know many mature children. Age does not guarantee maturity; maturity is not limited to adults. As it is with people, so it is with businesses. A business that is young in age can behave with maturity just as a business that has existed for many years can become stuck in a state of immaturity.

As the story of Sam Walton reminds me, bad decisions are the seeds of learning, developing expertise and ability. Said another way, you can't become a good horseman until you've fallen off the horse. Complexity drives maturity, and maturity explicitly defines the way suicide, if it is to occur, will be manifested. This concept is described by the Arc of Success, which is defined more fully in chapter 3, "The Problems with Success."

Chapters 4–11 explore the eight aforementioned components of purpose, performance, and people in greater detail. I'll explain how to create and use them, who is responsible for them, their durability, and examples of good and bad. In chapter 12, I'll explain how to apply my findings and turn the subjective aspects of this book into objective measures of success and sustainability.

CHAPTER 3

The Problems with Success

Organizations have lifecycles… They go through the normal struggles and difficulties accompanying growth and are faced with the transitional problems of moving from one phase of development to the next. Organizations learn to deal with these problems by themselves or they develop abnormal "diseases" that stymie growth.

—Ichak Adizes[11]

Like the prizefighter who doesn't see the punch coming, a business can be knocked out by unexpected change fueled by success. As the inescapable catalyst for failure, every organization will learn to manage change for its benefit, or fail.

Experience provides the ability to recognize early signs of an imminent change (risk event) and react properly. When bubbles begin to form on the bottom of a saucepan, you know the water is about to boil. When you hear thunder and see lightning, you know rain is likely. Likewise, when you can anticipate impending change,

---

[11] Introduction. 1989. In 1140850128 859046951 I. Adizes (author), *Corporate Lifecycles: How and Why Corporations Grow and Die and What to Do about It* (p. xiii). Englewood Cliffs, NJ: Prentice Hall.

you know a period of increased risk is coming that needs to be mitigated with planning and preparation.

Regrettably, the nature of business failure is unmerciful, and developing experience is expensive and traumatic.

> **"One of the primary objectives of this book is to replace the experience of failure with foresight so business suicide can be avoided."**

One of the primary objectives of this book is to replace the experience of failure with foresight so business suicide can be avoided. This chapter introduces the Arc of Success, which identifies the five phases of maturation every successful business will repeatedly go through.

The anecdote below chronicles the journey of a successful technology firm struggling with the growing pains of adolescence.

Mike's Anecdote
Everything Was Going So Well

Awake before the sun came up, I was energized and eager to get to the office. Wallace, our facilities manager and one of our first employees, was waiting for me at 6:08 just as I walked in. Wallace followed me into my office, saying, "Mike, am I still a trusted member of this team?" He didn't look happy.

Wallace is a great guy, smart, capable, dedicated, treats the business like it was his own. His weakness is his blue-collar attitude in a white-collar service world.

"That's a pretty harsh welcome at this hour of the morning, and borderline insulting," I responded as I sat at my desk. "What are you so upset about?"

Wallace was hotter than I realized, and his temperature was rising. He took a deep breath, rolled up his sleeves, put his hands on my desk, and leaned forward until we were almost nose to nose.

"Michael…"

He never calls me Michael.

"When I leave you a message, don't have one of your girls tell me who I'm supposed to be talking to. I'm not some newbie you've stuck into that chain of command you seem so eager to hide behind!"

Suddenly I understood. One of his workers had an accident claim the day before, and Wallace wanted to talk to me about it. My secretary, Rochelle, picked up my messages and told Wallace he needed to call our risk manager, not me. Wallace didn't know I would have told him the same thing if he'd been able to reach me.

After I spent my first hour and a half talking Wallace down and explaining the situation, he went to talk to Stephen, our risk manager. The parade wasn't over.

The instant Wallace stepped out of my office, our VP of sales and customer service, Peter, who had been standing outside my office waiting, ominously slid into the threshold of my door. It was 7:50, and I could feel my day starting to slip away.

"Mike, we're spending a fortune and busting our butts to make sales, and we're doing a pretty damn good job of it, if I must say so."

"Of course we are, Peter, your team has been kicking butt. They're the reason we finally hit $30 million." Peter was not surprised or happy.

"Got an email late last night from the parish executive down in Louisiana. He canceled the contract they signed six months ago. A five-year ten-million-dollar project. Gone, just like that."

"What?" I cried, "That was a sweet deal for them! What happened? Did he say what the problem was?" Now I was getting nervous.

"Mike," Peter explained, "I've been warning you about this problem for over a year now. You know it takes months to install one of our systems. Sales are doing a great job, but my installation people can't keep up, and it's not a simple fix. You can't throw money at the problem even if we have the money to throw. We got Louisiana excited and left them at the altar. They just got tired of waiting. Sorry to say it, but this isn't the first sale I think we're going to lose."

It took me another hour and a half just to get all the details. Peter was right; we'd sold too many systems too fast and weren't going to be able to deliver on our promises. This was a big problem.

By the time Peter left, my head was swimming. Meredith, our sales manager, came in seconds later. I'd been at work for four hours with nothing to show for it except anxiety and exhaustion.

"*You* screwed up, Mike" were the first words out of her mouth. With a throbbing ache from my neck to my legs, the day was heading toward a full meltdown. "Remember last month when you took the COO from the city of Stockton out for lunch?"

"Of course, and?"

"Remember where you went to lunch?"

"Meredith," I implored, "get to the point, please. I had a rough start today, and I'm already feeling beaten and bruised."

"Okay." She began. "You implemented a new expense policy at the beginning of our fiscal year four and a half months ago. So how much did you spend on lunch for you and Mr. Stockton COO?"

"Oh god, no." I knew what happened. The success of our marketing had led to a lot more sales calls and entertainment costs. Finance suggested we put a cap on the amount salespeople could spend when prospects and clients were entertained. The COO from Stockton likes wine, and he likes to drink at lunch. I'd overspent our new entertainment limit by a lot and apparently really hurt our sales team.

"Yup." Meredith looked at me. "One of my salespeople just got slapped around pretty good for being such a cheapskate. Mentioned your lunch with their boss. It sounded pretty ugly."

My morning that began with energy and enthusiasm had unexpectedly turned into a nightmare. After the inauspicious start, I needed some quiet time to compose myself and think.

The worst part was, these were all problems I could have, no, should have seen coming. Every one of these issues would have been avoided if I'd taken the time to look, process, and mitigate the impact our growth was having on our staff. It was actually somewhat demoralizing.

It's been difficult for me to remember that I need to be more careful now. We've gotten to the point where my actions can create problems for staff, and I really should think long and hard about new policies and procedures. This isn't fun anymore; this is work. I missed the days of our small team in our small office trying to give birth to our new tech firm. We had big ideas. Now I feel like I'm sticking my leg out and tripping the team up every time I act. This has to change; I have to change.

The Arc of Success

Similar in design to Kübler-Ross's five stages of grief,[12] the Arc of Success (Arc) foretells how the maturation process progresses at each stage of maturity. It can help organizations prepare for and manage the inevitable growing pains of success: pain that should be embraced, not feared or avoided.

Phase 0: New ideas

Each stage of maturity begins with new ideas. For youth, start-ups are routinely launched by innovators and entrepreneurs brimming with new ideas to pursue. Adolescence begins with new ideas about standards, best practices, and focus. Adulthood begins with new ideas about ways to connect, communicate, and engage. Each stage should also generate a regular stream of ideas on growth. New ideas are drivers of change.

Unfortunately, most unused new idea pipelines tend to remain clogged or closed. Stimulating ideas and helping an organization embrace change can be done with regular discussions of ways to improve. Creating idea flow takes minimal time and effort coupled with tolerance (for bad ideas) and a penalty-free environment.[13] When ideas flow, they're evaluated, implemented, or become projects and tend to generate some form of growth.

---

[12] Kübler-Ross, E., and Kessler, D. (2005). *On Grief and Grieving: Finding the Meaning of Grief through the Five Stages of Loss.* New York: Scribner.

[13] "A penalty-free environment is when an individual can try something new and different without the risk of doing damage or looking foolish." Mandelberg, Larry "Penalty-free Environment Provides Safe Haven for Training," *Sacramento Business Journal, American City Business Journals,* 3 September 2006, https://www.bizjournals.com/sacramento/stories/2006/09/04/smallb3.html.

Phase 1: Growth

As a breath of air is to the living, growth is the oxygen of business. A business that isn't growing is dying; it has effectively signed up for the business suicide installment plan. All paths that lead to success involve some aspect of growth.

Growth can be pursued in many forms beyond sales and profits. Products, services, markets served, and geographic reach are examples. Growth is a driver of change.

The issue Peter faced in the anecdote above was that the company had outsold its capacity to deliver and was unable to fulfill the customer expectations they'd set. New customers were showing signs of impatience, and the firm didn't have the ability to solve the problem even though Mike and the VP of sales and customer service eventually saw it coming.

Additional predictable changes created by growth include the need to:

- Manage new customers;
- Acquire new or additional resources (e.g., equipment, facilities, etc.);
- Hire, train, and manage staff; and
- Ensure workloads remain realistic, balanced, and able to handle the growth.

A Business that Isn't Growing Is Dying

The recurring need to explain this maxim is always a surprise to me. The simplest explanation I've come across goes like this: if you never grow your customer base, eventually they will all die, and you'll have no customers.

As you may expect, that isn't typically good enough for naysayers. A more technically appropriate logic goes like this: If change is constant, the value of everything your organization delivers is subject to change. Since time moves forward and change tends to look forward while leaving the past behind, the value of your unchanging products and services to your static customer base is more likely to decrease than increase. If you're not routinely looking for new products, services, customers, or ways to deliver value, over time, your business won't have anything valuable to offer.

When taken too literally by those naysayers, the point quickly gets lost; it doesn't stop being true. A business that isn't growing is dying. Or, as I prefer to say, they've signed up for the business suicide installment plan.

Phase 2: Complexity

Imagine the simplest business you can think of—a business that sells one product to one buyer. A small coffee shop selling freshly brewed coffee would be a good example.

If our simple business is successful, it will acquire new customers with individual needs and wants—dark roast or light, decaf or regular, cream and sugar or black, flavored, iced—each one a variable that impacts the business relationship with each customer. Once our simple business begins offering options to customers, the complexity of each transaction quickly multiplies even though we're still just selling freshly brewed coffee. Complexity is a driver of change.

Customer demands and the desire to serve them lead to specialized expertise, capabilities, and departments to support them. Serving more customers requires more salespeople and support staff. When our simple business expands to multiple locations, varied local, state, and federal regulations must be identified and adhered to. Many aspects of growth bring numerous additional variables.

In the anecdote above, the risks associated with workplace accidents required specialized knowledge the boss, Mike, didn't have. The facilities manager was upset with the new chain of command and hadn't been properly prepared.

Additional predictable changes created by complexity include:

- Interdependence between products and services;
- More frequent decisions with greater impact creating greater risks;
- New skills and knowledge to sell, support, and manage new products and services;
- Delegation to make sure everything gets done; and
- Economies of scale to maintain service levels.

Phase 3: Controls

As complexity grows, cross-departmental coordination becomes increasingly significant. Effective business development requires coordination of public relations, marketing, and sales product development, manufacturing, distribution, installation, and support. Communication protocols need to be put in place to ensure the appropriate people have the appropriate information at the appropriate times.

Policies and procedures become necessary, and delegation becomes essential. Staff development and succession planning need to be integrated into operations as decisions become more critical, time-consuming, and frequent. Enhanced management skills to support an increasingly diverse staff and their responsibilities become vital. Controls are a driver of change.

In the anecdote above, Meredith was forced to confront arbitrary compliance with policy. When a new policy was implemented to control costs, the boss, Mike, failed to comply. The sales manager and her staff were embarrassed, and the company looked bad.

Additional predictable changes created by controls include the following:

- Economies of scale limit special treatment for individual clients;
- Delegation requires adjustment of authority to ensure delegated responsibilities can be achieved;
- The learning curve for implementing new rules, guidelines, policies, and procedures impacts everyone's ability to perform their duties;
- Unexpected obstacles slow down the normal course of business;
- "Chain of Command" communication is needed to ensure proper implementation.

Phase 4: Diminished flexibility

Controls are an inescapable aspect of growth and can feel different, depending on one's perspective. For some, controls feel like straitjackets or roadblocks that should be avoided. For others, controls provide clarity, confidence, and guidance.

Diminished flexibility impacted all three of the managers in our anecdote. As controls become more pervasive, they must be regularly reviewed and carefully evaluated to ensure they're doing more good than harm. When controls begin to create more problems than they prevent, they need to be reconceived along with a review of organizational structure. Diminished flexibility is a driver of change.

Additional predictable changes created by diminished flexibility include the following:

- Value propositions evolve, requiring timely and precise communication to internal and external stakeholders;
- Adjustments to staff responsibilities to ensure they are aligned with individual authority and avoid conflicts with policies and procedures;
- Serving customers outside the target market becomes increasingly difficult, time-consuming, and costly;
- Extraordinary client requests become harder to accommodate.

Diminished flexibility at the end of each Arc cycle can rapidly turn negative. From an external perspective, planning and efforts to inform stakeholders and communicate value become harder and more crucial. From an internal perspective, *change driven by success created by a talented staff doing good work can easily lead to a toxic environment for those who helped create it.*[14]

*****

In preadulthood organizations, toxicity arising from journeying through the Arc marks the end of a culture and way of doing business. It also opens a gateway to the next stage and another journey through the Arc. For youth, the focus must shift from finding purpose to figuring out how to consistently deliver value. For adolescence, the focus must shift from consistent performance to creating engagement of people across growing spectra of geographic and socioeconomic variables.

---

[14] See "Growing pain no. 2: Good behavior becomes bad" below.

Adulthood embodies growth in size,[15] experience, and human capital. Survival in this stage depends on continued fulfillment of the first two Ps. Only then can leadership and the organization begin to develop and nourish true engagement of staff, the third P, people.

The threat to survival at this stage is losing the connection between an organization's decision makers and its customers. As the number of staff between these two groups grows, customers' changing needs and wants become increasingly difficult to identify. Over time, the wants and needs of your market tend to shift. Failing to identify these changes sows the seeds of self-destruction. These self-destructive seeds flourish when the organization fails to adapt.

Can a business survive without change?

> *"The question is not whether your business is going to change; the questions are, what changes will your business face tomorrow, how will your business adapt to them, and will it be in time?"*

No.
The question is not whether your business is going to change; the questions are, what changes will your business face tomorrow, how will your business adapt to them, and will it be in time? The key to answering those questions requires foresight and the ability to recognize when change is needed.

---

[15] Size in this context includes products and services, customers, service area, and the staff to deliver and support them.

The three most common signs of the need for change are the following growing pains.

1. symptoms masquerading as root problems,
2. historically good operational behaviors that begin to create undesirable results, and
3. emotional resistance to beneficial change.

Growing pain no. 1: Symptoms masquerading as root problems

One of the most common occurrences in the workplace is interruption. Whether everyday activities or special projects, work is routinely derailed by interruptions demanding attention. These disruptions can be like unpleasant odors you can't get rid of.

The frequent reaction is to let yourself be distracted by trying to resolve interruptions of lesser importance in the moment even though you know the disruptions *never* seem to get resolved. These disturbances often trigger an unjustified sense of urgency that diverts you from higher priorities. The most detrimental aspect, and the reason these speed bumps never go away, is *because they're symptoms, not the cause*, of deeper issues.

The time and money invested in trying to fix these symptoms distract from the demands of running a business, not to mention potential opportunity costs.

My father and I shared that sense of frustration with the attention-grabbing problems that seem to arise all too often. As a constant reminder, he had a full-page ad from the *Wall Street Journal* framed and hung on his office wall—a picture of a rock and a slingshot that looked like something David would have used in the ninth century BC to slay Goliath. At the bottom, it said, "Goliath was killed by an assumption."

I don't remember who that ad was for because I never heard my father mention the name of the company that placed it even though he repeated its tagline habitually.

I've had numerous firsthand experiences helping my clients recognize symptoms masquerading as root problems. One of my favorites was the case of the assistants who wouldn't stay.

Background information. One of the top-producing partners in a law firm with hundreds of lawyers lost his assistant of many years to retirement.

Issue definition. After five attempts in eighteen months, securing a new assistant for him had been unsuccessful. Exit interviews with these disgruntled replacements revealed their hasty departures were due to the partner, whom they consistently characterized as difficult or impossible to work with.

Strategic impact. The other partners were faced with two high-impact problems. Terminate the partner and lose his revenue and clients or risk a harassment lawsuit, which could be more damaging and costly.

Ideal outcome. The partner's next assistant would become a valued resource and support him for many years.

Action plan. Hire a coach to "fix" the partner, avoid his termination, and reduce the risk of a lawsuit. That's what the board hired me to do.

As I began working with the partner, I quickly realized his personality was part of the problem. Changing someone's personality typically requires a life-threatening event or exposure to some form of extreme trauma. An interesting example of this is a nurse my wife met when she was admitted to the trauma ward of a hospital. My wife asked the nurse how she was able to cope with an environment of continuous trauma.

The nurse explained she'd been raised in an abusive family and had spent her entire life surrounded by trauma, so this job was comfortable and familiar to her. She knew how to cope because she learned how to survive it as a child. As unhealthy as it might have been, the nurse was unable to shake her need to be surrounded by trauma.

This partner had been working with his longtime assistant doing the same work for many years, and his management style hadn't suddenly changed. After much distressing reflection and honest discussion, the problem came into clear focus.

Human resources was using the firm's "standard" legal assistant-skills profile to find his replacement. Clearly, it wasn't working. The personality traits this attorney needed in his assistant—concise, direct, unequivocal—were significantly different from HR's model candidate—pleasant, patient, and compassionate. Any candidate who fit the recruitment profile was never going to solve this problem. The only meaningful solution was to customize the recruitment profile for this partner, which could lead to everyone wanting the same freedom to recruit outside the boundaries.

The thought of changing a process appearing to have worked so well for years was disconcerting to the board and felt disruptive to HR. They feared change and the destabilizing impact it might have on the organization. No one was happy with my proposed solution except the partner and me. After further uncomfortable discussion and thoughtful consideration by the board and head of HR, it was agreed we would try creating some flexibility in the hiring profile. The next assistant they hired for the partner worked well and stayed with him for the duration of his tenure with the law firm.

What first appeared to be an abusive attorney ended up being more like locking a dog who doesn't like cats in a cage with a cat who doesn't like dogs and expecting them to get along. The root problem was HR's recruitment process.

When disruption, problems, or issues arise, it's critical to the progress and development of all aspects of an organization for its leaders to separate symptoms from problems, solve them, and avoid playing Whack-A-Mole.

Growing pain no. 2: Historically good operational behaviors that begin to create undesirable results

With homage to Ralph Waldo Emerson, Oliver Goldsmith, Arthur Ashe, and likely numerous others, success is a journey, not a destination. The more you prepare for it, the more likely you will survive its pitfalls and enjoy both the journey and your achievements.

An organization's success is fueled by behaviors and activities that create positive results. When those behaviors begin having no impact or, worse, negative impact, letting go of them is often difficult.

This client case study explores the insidious nature of this problem and demonstrates how it becomes unwelcome barnacles putting a drag on success.

Background information. An entrepreneurial venture came to life in 1998 to serve specific educational needs of children and their parents. Over the next twenty years, this 501(c)(3) California nonprofit public benefit corporation grew to over five hundred employees serving as many as eight thousand students. The organization was (unknowingly) completing the second cycle of the Arc of Success and transitioning from adolescence into adulthood.

Issue definition. Most of the operations' staff were experiencing the cultural shift inherent in organizational maturation for the first time. The friction created by transitioning into the third cycle of the Arc was creating frustration and decreasing morale. That's when I was hired.

Strategic impact. Their positive, collaborative workplace was at risk of becoming a toxic, competitive environment where working relationships, developed over decades, could be undermined.

Ideal outcome. Create a better understanding of the new normal and why it was a healthy, expected result of their success. Help staff make the transition and embrace it while avoiding turnover.

Action plan. Educate staff on the impacts of success. Show them how their hard work and efforts were the reason for their success. Get everyone refocused on the future, leave the past behind, and continue moving toward the organization's vision.

This was a problem that both management and staff were ill-prepared for. Neither had sufficient experience to anticipate or solve it. Management had not prepared staff for the inevitable changes taking place in part because they hadn't anticipated them while operational demands kept everyone busy.

The first symptoms appeared when staff began resisting the chain of command. Many felt they were working in a democracy rather than a collaborative business with well-defined controls.

Once the team understood the burdens that come with growth, they began to change their perspective. An appreciation for what they helped create emerged, and their focus shifted to looking for ways to collectively identify and solve the problems they were sure to encounter.

What began with the feel of an impending insurgency became a new understanding that brought people closer together. Some staff left, and targeted operational changes were made. Rather than being resentful of new controls and decreased flexibility, they took pride in the success of the organization and embraced their responsibility to sustain it.

Having the emotional capacity to look forward with eager anticipation and avoid looking back at lost freedom is critical to surviving in a constantly changing environment. Without the ability to adapt, no organization or the people within it can survive.

Good behavior and processes can become unproductive or counterproductive with little warning. Of the three growing pains, *this is often the most challenging to identify or correct.* It's difficult to change how we do things; changing how productive and appreciated employees do their work is tougher. When traditionally accepted practices start creating problems, it's time for new, different, and unfamiliar standards to be implemented.

Growing pain no. 3: Emotional resistance to beneficial change

The changes people usually like are the changes they do unto others. The changes people often dislike and resist are the changes done unto them *by* others. It's difficult to implement change until people are willing to see its benefits and accept its inevitability. Only then can they embrace those benefits and contribute to the business pursuits.

In this chapter's opening anecdote when Wallace had a problem, he knew that Mike, his friend and boss, had always helped him handle it. Given the company's growth, Mike didn't have sufficient expertise or time to deal with HR problems. Wallace's reliance on Mike had to change.

Now, when closing new customers, Peter's sales staff had to consider other departments within the company that contributed to the success of each sale. The way prospects were recruited and converted to customers had to change.

When Meredith's sales team was undermined by Mike and his failure to follow the newly implemented policy, the company looked bad. Mike's subconscious sense of entitlement and disregard for his need to conform to company policies, like everyone else, had to change.

What follows is one of my most compelling examples of this growing pain.

Background information. A twenty-year-old healthcare services firm had suddenly grown gross sales 400 percent and staff 250 percent. Their services were substantial contributors to healthy communities, and demand was at an all-time high.

Issue definition. In spite of their success and growth, over the course of a three-year period, the firm suffered its first operating losses. They began with a $300,000 net loss. The next year, they had an additional loss of $500,000. The following year began on pace to lose $800,000. That's when the CEO engaged me.

Strategic impact. Failure to change the current trajectory would lead to the financial collapse of the firm. The communities they served would lose their primary source for the services my client was providing.

Ideal outcome. Identify the root problem and return to profitability while continuing to sustainably serve these critical needs and implement appropriate changes to avoid this problem in the future.

Action plan. Transition the firm's leadership team struggling to escape youth into adolescence and facilitate the development of a foundation designed to help them continue maturing while growing profitably.

Prior to digging into this problem, external third parties had verified there was no underlying fraud or wrongdoing. We began with a thorough review of operations and identified numerous customers whose needs were on the fringes of my client's core strengths.

Efforts to serve them were costly, unprofitable, and time-consuming, negatively impacting operational activities.

These unsuitable customers were organizations with varied and substantial needs my client had the skills to fulfill. What my client lacked was the capacity and organizational structure to do so properly or profitably. This presented substantial moral and ethical dilemmas.

My client's services were appropriately priced. Saying no to organizations in need and able to pay felt wrong. Given the context of their environment, raising prices would be inappropriate and a short-term fix at best. The only sustainable solution was to limit services to prospects they had the capacity to properly serve until they could increase it without losing quality or dependability.

We debated this solution for several weeks while looking for alternatives. Eventually, it became clear to everyone that we'd exhausted all reasonable arguments and it was time for this team to face reality. What first looked like successful growth ended up nearly bankrupting the firm and was more poisonous than beneficial. If they didn't start saying no to people in need, they were going to go broke.

The leadership team agreed to create and implement guidelines and stop contracting for projects they hadn't developed the capacity to properly serve. Determining the requisite criteria for new clients was difficult and stressful. Each team member, including the CEO, had exceptions they felt were inviolable. When they finally realized that avoiding this change meant going out of business and serving no one, they succumbed.

My client had been struggling to advance past the youth stage of maturity. They had been reluctant to say no to prospects in need and unable to shift their focus from fulfilling their purpose to delivering consistent performance. Internal operations and the quality and dependability of their services suffered greatly.

Roles and responsibilities were revised, and guidelines were put in place with controls to monitor and ensure compliance. A few members of the leadership team resigned. Some clients were upset; others, disappointed. Eventually, the unprofitable and costly clients were phased out, quality of service was restored, and profits returned.

*****

Friction and discomfort are normal symptoms of healthy growth in a business just as they are in a child. You can't stop change unless you stop aging, and the only way to do that is to stop living. When change is seen in the proper light, it can stimulate energy and creativity.

Change is not a question of if, but how and when. Change for the right reasons is a beautiful thing. The ability to deal with change effectively is the difference between success and failure. If you avoid it for too long, you might lose everything.

Key Points

Ch 1	Operational Imperatives	Clarity of purpose	Consistency of performance	Engagement of people
Ch 2	Stage of Maturity	Youth	Adolescence	Adulthood
Ch 2	Why leaders fail to achieve the 3 P's.	They didn't know they needed to do them.	They didn't know how to do them.	They forgot they needed to do them.
Ch 3	Arc of Success	New Ideas ▶ Growth ▶ Complexity ▶ Controls ▶ Less Flexibility		
Ch 3	Problems with Success	Symptoms masquerading as root problems	Historically good operational behaviors begin creating undesirable results	Emotional resistance to beneficial change
Ch 3	Index Indicators & (chapter #)	Values Vision Mission	Business Plan Marketing Plan Goals and Responsibilities	Systems and Structure Communications Plan

One of the primary objectives of this book is to replace the experience of failure with foresight so business suicide can be avoided.

The Arc of Success foretells the five phases of change business experience as they progress through each stage of maturity.

As with people, organizations experience growing pains as they mature. The three most common are

- symptoms masquerading as root problems,
- historically good operational behaviors that begin to create undesirable results, and
- emotional resistance to logically beneficial change.

A business that's not growing is dying.

PART 2

YOUTH AND THE FIRST P: CLARITY OF PURPOSE

Identifying your organization's purpose reeks of irony. Purpose is often the first thing leadership is clear about. The irony lies in the difficulty documenting it, which is typically the most time-consuming guidance offered here.

An organization without a consistently and clearly expressed purpose is like a ship without a rudder, meandering without direction in a sea of possibilities. Lack of clarity of purpose is the primary cause of business failure (suicide) for organizations in youth, the first stage of maturity. As such, the three fundamental indicators defining purpose—values, vision, and mission—become the most critical, foundational *must-haves* of every organization.

Many roll their eyes at the mere mention of any of the purpose statements. The opinion held by too many is, values, vision, and mission statements are too touchy-feely and have little worth. They are right for the wrong reasons. Half-baked, poorly written, improperly deployed values, vision, or mission statements are worse than worthless; they're harmful.

CHAPTER 4

The Cultural Framework:
Values Statements

Index Indicator #1

Values statements are the first of eight leading Index indicators of organizational success and sustainability. They facilitate clarity of purpose. They describe what it feels like to work with you and for you. They should parrot what your customers say about you when asked, "Why do you do business with them?" Good values statements should also reflect the core beliefs of the founders.

An organization needs values because the only way there can be any real control over the culture of your organization and the behavior of your staff is by defining, promoting, encouraging, and measuring the behaviors that align with the culture you want in your company.

It is through the explicit implementation of a values-based filter for all activities within your company that the culture you want can be created, nourished, and thrive.

Culture, when properly developed and maintained, will feed and successfully guide the business in fulfilling its mission and achieving its vision. Values are the behavioral guidelines and ethical boundaries of every business. Create and implement values statements and your business will begin its course toward long-term success.

The biggest problem I see with values statements is when those most critical to their embrace, leadership, give them little more than lip service. When staff and customers can't see company values in

70

leadership decisions or behaviors, it's unrealistic to expect either to respect or be guided by them. Ignoring your stated values can be more hazardous than not having any values at all.

> *"ignoring your stated values can be more hazardous than not having any values at all."*

The Enron lesson

Enron's values as presented in their 1999 annual report to shareholders.

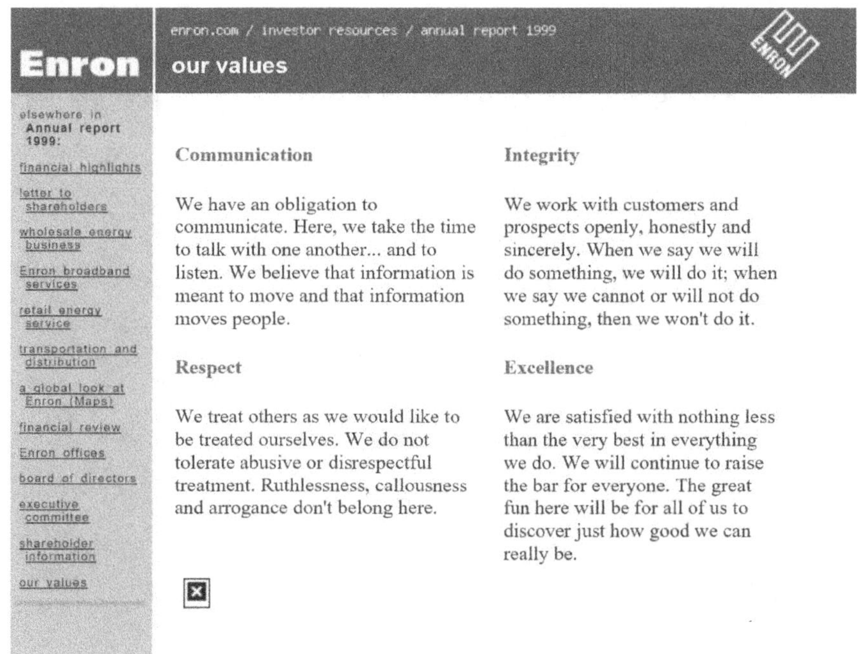

An outstanding set of values statements that, based on a rear-view mirror perspective of the company's failure, weren't properly implemented. They became instructions on how not to behave, toxic smoke screens for conceit and abuse festering within the company.

With a few word changes, what follows is a more accurate representation of how I believe their values led to Enron's culture:

- *Communications.* We have an obligation to *avoid communication.* Here, we *do not* take the time to talk with one another…or to listen. We believe that information is meant *to be hidden* and that information *stops* people.
- *Integrity.* We work *against* customers and prospects *covertly, dishonestly,* and *insincerely.* When we say we will do something, we *won't* do it; when we say we cannot or will not do something, then we *will* do it.
- *Respect.* We *do not* treat others as we would like to be treated ourselves. We tolerate abusive or disrespectful treatment. Ruthlessness, callousness, and arrogance *do* belong here.
- *Excellence.* We are satisfied with nothing less than the very *least* in everything we do. We will continue to *lower* the bar for everyone. The great fun here will be for all of us to discover just how *rich* we can really be.

Enron demonstrated how values that are unused, disrespected, or ignored can be suicidal in a stark and financially devastating manner. *Enron's failure in this one area became their undoing.* The result was an indelible example of how unfulfilled commitments became good words that worked against them and destroyed the lives of many people.

Benefits of Values Statements

Your beliefs become your thoughts. Your thoughts become your words. Your words become your actions. Your actions become your habits. Your habits become your values. Your values become your destiny.

—Mahatma Gandhi[16]

Values are inherent in the very nature of being human. Every business has a human element. Every human has values, whether they're explicitly stated and recognized or not. Therefore, every business has values, whether they're known and staff is aligned with them or not.

> "every business has values, whether they're known and staff is aligned with them or not."

Identifying company values reduces risk. Creating values statements delineates the work environment. Implementing them establishes behavioral norms. Inculcating staff to them creates its culture. Actively embracing them in daily operations makes them real.

Not doing so endorses inaccurate perceptions and assumptions about what they mean and how to adhere to them.

In the absence of a culture that understands and embraces its organizational values, the business will emulate the values of the most dominant individuals within it. Inconsistencies among those individuals will take the business out of alignment and have painful consequences.

---

[16] Gandhi. "Mahatma Gandhi > Quotes > Quotable Quote," *Goodreads*. https://www.goodreads.com/quotes/50584-your-beliefs-become-your-thoughts-your-thoughts-become-your-words.

The need for behavioral norms can and must be defined by each organization, not society in general, if the organization has any chance of success and sustainability. The mere act of identifying and documenting the values you want to be embraced and emulated provides every thinking person the guidelines within which they are expected to behave and conduct themselves.

Creating, documenting, and implementing company values has seven primary benefits: company culture, trust, engagement, retention, marketing, recruiting, and decision-making.

Company culture

Working collaboratively with others throughout an organization is often a major component of success. As staff diversity increases, a thorny blend of cultures arise. As management of those cultures becomes more difficult, profitability and, often, survival become dependent on engineering, implementing, and maintaining a common company culture.

When the values of your company are clearly defined, you'll have a template for the culture you need to create. With proper implementation and reinforcement, your culture will become self-sustaining. It will accept those who fit and reject those who don't.

A good culture can lead to trust.

Trust

Saying what you'll do and doing what you say is part of the basis for trust.

One of my greatest frustrations with the companies I work with as a vendor, customer, or contractor is when they fail to meet my expectations. When I do my research and am told what to expect, I want them to fulfill the expectations they set for me.

It takes multiple positive referrals to create trust and only one negative to make prospects wary. When I research a vendor online, I look for the negative reviews because I want to know if they've failed to meet the expectations they've set for their customers.

Trust allows for engagement.

Engagement

I passionately believe the most valuable asset any company has is its employees. In the field of human resources, employee engagement is occasionally described as the employer's holy grail.[17] An engaged workforce is less wasteful, has lower turnover, and communicates better, which leads to greater profit.

When an employee is not engaged, they're not contributing to the overall success of the company. They are essentially being paid more for what they are doing than their counterparts who are more engaged and productive. The unengaged exist as tumors within the organization, ripe for making mistakes and sowing seeds of discontent.

Engagement creates a sense of attachment, which leads to retention.

Retention

Most people remember their worst job, typically described as having an uncomfortable or difficult work environment. Research has proven most people leave their jobs because of a bad manager or hostile work environment, not because of compensation. From the smallest mom-and-pop shop to the largest high-tech corporations, employees come and go because of the way they're treated at work.

When you and I have common values, we automatically have common ground. When issues, problems, or conflicts arise in the course of doing business, common ground can provide the opportunity for people on opposite sides of these situations to find points of connection and talk. The more aligned the values of everyone involved in the process, the more likely they will be to find common ground.

Common ground is how relationships are developed. Common ground is how partnerships are built. Common ground is what makes collaboration work. We can respect one another and enjoy working together. Enjoyment creates an emotional draw and attracts people.

Attracting people to a business is the role of marketing.

---

[17] See the section titled *Adulthood and the Third P: Engagement of People* on page 172.

Marketing

Your best marketing lives in demonstrated values you're proud of, a workforce that is engaged and productive, and clients whose expectations are routinely met; these are priceless assets. Being connected to them and sharing them makes everyone in the company proud while creating desire for increased internal and external participation.

That desire to be a part of something good, fun, and successful almost makes recruiting easy.

Recruiting

When your firm has a reputation for having a great culture, being trustworthy, and having engaged employees that have been there a long time, other people want to join with you. Recruiting is already expensive, difficult, and risky. It becomes much cheaper, easier, and less speculative when you have prequalified candidates who are clear on why they want to work for your firm, eager to do so, and actively coming to you.

The benefits outlined above also play a role in staff selection (i.e., prospective colleagues). A healthy, positive environment driven by a happy, productive workforce will, over time, reject individuals in conflict with it. In short, if you want to play with us, you need to fit in and contribute. When that happens, your staff has begun to learn how to be less dependent on a manager and more self-reliant.

When values statements are in place and the benefits outlined above are being experienced, they create consistencies that tend to minimize the most difficult decisions.

Decision-making

Making decisions is the most common and frequent activity of every employee of every business. When choices and their benefits are clear, decisions are easier. When staff are expected to read the boss's mind, not so much. Values statements and the stories that demonstrate their application are the easiest and fastest way to communicate and inculcate each value.

The ability to provide insight into what the values mean helps staff make better decisions and improves the likelihood customers, vendors, and employees will consistently have realistic expectations. In the conflict between want and need, values often reduce the emotional tug of short-term benefit and help maintain focus on the future. This type of clarity is how leadership begins to add "value through values" to every company stakeholder, including themselves.

Why ignore the benefits of embracing values statements when they're free and can improve so many aspects of your business?

Britt's Anecdote
The Case of the Plagued Patriarch

In the seventeen months since joining the firm, Britt Poole was no stranger to the room—an environment she was certain had been designed to intimidate. The regal cherrywood table, leather-bound books, high-back chairs, and scent of power generated pheromones that seemed to warn every interloper; here lives a presence to be reckoned with.

Poole entered the room to find founding partner, Willard Kronick, and his five power partners seated in their decreed places along with a dozen or so attorneys looking primed and ready for court. Yet something was different, and she could feel it the moment she came in for this morning's ad hoc meeting. An unfamiliar presence of uncertainty was in this familiar place with familiar faces—the conference room of Sanborne, Hollande, and Kronick.

After forty years of hard work, all the pieces were finally falling into place and the firm was growing like a weed. Their decades of success and legal experience had made SHK one of the most respected in town. In the last two years, staff had expanded from 65 to over 250. It sounded great and felt terrible.

The rapid growth had given rise to a certain loss of control, and for attorneys, that's never a good thing. An uncomfortable, unfamiliar feeling lurked throughout the dark corners of their offices. They couldn't tell if a grain of sand had found its way into their oyster and was making a pearl or the firm was about to implode. Either way, it felt prickly, and Britt could tell she was about to be forced to face it head-on.

"I'm troubled," the patriarch opened the meeting. "I'm distressed by our rapid growth. It feels like we're growing too fast, and I'm worried about our reputation. I know growth is critical, but it feels like all these new people are putting us at risk. How are we going to make sure we don't endanger our reputation?"

Randy Schneider, one of the firm's most successful partners, was visibly bothered by Kronick's comments.

"Willard, our clients are thrilled, and we're having our best year ever, yet I'm feeling a lot of anxiety. What is going on?"

"Randy," Kronick said, "it's times like this when everything seems to be humming along that I worry the most. I feel I'm missing something. A law firm doesn't succeed just because it's providing good counsel. How we do business, our values, our ethics, how we treat our clients, these things can get away from us. When our growth exceeds our ability to manage it, we're in trouble."

The managing partner, Martin Grange, responded, "Walter, I see no evidence of a problem. Has HR given you any reason to be concerned? It's not like you to raise an issue like this out of the blue. I'm not seeing or hearing anything from staff or clients that worries me. What do you see the rest of us aren't seeing?"

"What kind of support and oversight is happening with our new people?" Kronick answered. "Can anybody in this room tell me they know whether our new staff is even capable of representing us the way we want to be represented?"

Bob Gaiety was generally considered their most successful and respected rainmaker. If anybody should be concerned, Bob would be that guy.

"Willard," Gaiety began, "I do not have your level of concern. It doesn't sound like you're worried about a problem with our new people. It sounds like you want proof we can handle our growth without losing who we are and what we stand for."

"That's exactly what I'm concerned about."

As the only one in this meeting who was part of the growth Willard was referring to, Britt felt everyone was waiting for her to say something. She wasn't quite sure how honest she could be.

"I'll admit, I was a bit lost when I started last year," she said to Kronick. "I was given all the history, how you, Sanborne, and Mr. Hollande began, and I was proud to be joining the firm. But once I came on board, I never felt like part of a team. Our values have always bothered me," she said.

"What?" Several people murmured while looking at one another with raised eyebrows.

"We have them posted all over the office," Britt explained, "but what exactly does teamwork mean? Does it mean my team does my busy work for me? What do reliability, trustworthiness, and transparency mean to you? And how are they supposed to affect the way I do my work, the way I interact with clients or our staff? How do I know if I'm doing it your way? How do any of us know if we have an accurate understanding of what you want from us?"

"Fair point," said Gaiety. "Not sure how we might be able to do that. If we could do it in a way that didn't make people feel like they were being watched, like big brother wasn't waiting to pounce on them for the tiniest slipup, if it could be done in a positive manner, I don't see how it would hurt."

Mary Sanchez, one of the more respected partners Britt didn't know very well, spoke up.

"I have a tech client that does something I've been intrigued by ever since I found out about it. They only have twenty-five or thirty people, so they're not as big as we are, and they have a company meeting every Monday for lunch. They serve pizza for everyone, employees and contractors, full- and part-time. When their vendors are in town, they're also welcome to join.

"They open the meeting by going down their list of values. They read each one and talk about it. I was there the other day when they brought up one about honesty. I think it reads, 'We value honesty.' After they read each values statement, people start telling stories about how they demonstrated that value during the week."

Mary took a moment to gather her thoughts. "I was there recently when a project manager for a multimillion-dollar project they were working on for a Fortune 50 firm, one of their bigger clients, told an honesty-value story he had been involved in. His project got behind schedule, and his entire development team was starting to stress out. The project manager went to the client and told them the moment he knew they were going to miss a deadline. This was way before any due dates had been missed, before there was any sign of trouble or delay. They just knew they weren't going to make the deadline and wanted the client to know as soon as possible."

Now the whole room was focused on Mary.

"Many of you know that's not the way IT firms operate," she said. "The common reaction is to wait until the deadline is missed, then tell the client there's going to be a delay. Not these guys. They were proud to be late, and I think it was because they had good reason. He told the story about their explanation for the delay and how the client reacted. The client was thrilled and couldn't believe the integrity shown in being up-front with them, making sure the delay didn't come as a surprise. It gave everyone time to analyze, review, and adjust. They revisited all the project milestones, renegotiated the elements that needed to be adjusted, and quickly got back on track, well before anything went south. It's not hard to imagine why that client has become a great referral source and a fierce supporter.

"Turns out, the way they manage their culture is by focusing on their values and making them come alive by sharing stories every week, by asking staff for examples of how those values are brought to life. The meaning of their values really comes to life when they're described through stories of daily activity.

"Maybe we should start doing something like that?" she offered.

Creating Your Values Statements

Creating values statements often appears deceivingly simple. As in the Taoist tradition, for every yin, there is a yang. The benefits of values statements represent the brightness and growth associated with the yang. The difficult and painful process of creating and implementing values statements is represented by the shadows and wave troughs associated with the yin. In time, the initial struggles of creation are balanced by calming the daily battle of business—the Taoist concept of balance that leads to harmony.

The simultaneous intersection of the growth and maturation of technology with the growth and maturation of millennials[18] has led to greater diversity in many cultural attributes (e.g., age, gender, religion, social status, and sexual orientation). Interaction with people who are not like you is becoming more frequent and common than ever before.

Traditional barriers that have kept diverse groups separated are deteriorating while creating a workplace that is unfamiliar to many, particularly those older and more experienced. This escalation of diversity, coupled with new modalities of human interaction, has never been greater or had more impact. The increased focus on how people interact has created a *new normal* for behavior at work. Values statements can be a powerful solution to help manage it.

Begin with a diverse group of people to brainstorm with the owners/leaders. Ask each person to close their eyes and think of someone they respect and admire, whether alive or dead, fictional or real, someone whose praise they would value. Ask them to silently identify why these specific individuals were selected, and list the values they are believed to embody. Put everyone's list of values on something big enough for everyone to see and start going through them.

While you may be able to list twenty "important" values, it's neither practical nor functional to include all of them. Anybody can remember three, and most can't remember more than seven; my research found four to six is ideal. If leadership cannot encompass the culture they want to create in seven values statements, they're not sufficiently clear or aligned.

One common facilitation technique I like is to begin by eliminating duplicates then grouping similar values until there are no more than seven groups. Select one value for each group, talk about what it means and how it can be demonstrated, then start building statements that explain how to live them. Once you have your statements, the group needs to prioritize them. Finally, everyone needs to

---

[18] Dimock, M. (2019, January 17), "Defining Generations: Where Millennials End and Generation Z Begins." Retrieved from http://www.pewresearch.org/fact-tank/2019/01/17/where-millennials-end-and-generation-z-begins/.

take a list away with them and think about each value and statement for at least a week. By then your team will be well on their way.

Two risks to be aware of include short-term value and groupthink.[19] First, values must be sustainable for a long period of time. The investment in behavioral development is too great and powerful for short-term viability. Second, it can be easy for a group to come together and convince themselves they are on the same page with a set of values only to find the group has engaged in groupthink.

Values statements must anticipate the unknown and provide guidance for questions that have yet to be asked and decisions that have yet to be made. Good ones represent beliefs the organization is unwilling, sometimes unable to sacrifice, in the pursuit and performance of its business activities.

In that light, values become the emotional, intellectual, and tactical guideposts everyone in your organization depends on to make decisions that are consistently aligned with the culture you want to develop, nurture, and maintain. Values statements can create a rock-solid foundation for growth and sustainability that can be built upon for many years, through change, turmoil, and troubles.

As part of the values development process, each organization must ensure its values statements align with the decorum, demeanor, and core tenets of the markets it serves and not be dictated by trends or variables that create market volatility. If they aren't, history shows us behavior will evolve with no concern for your organization's long-term health and welfare. It will be defined by the path of least resistance,[20] which is never the most efficacious.[21]

---

[19] Psychology Today. "What Is Groupthink?" Retrieved March 9, 2019. https://www.psychologytoday.com/us/basics/groupthink.

[20] Fritz, Robert. *The Path of Least Resistance*. 1st ed. New York, NY: Fawcett Columbine, 1989. Print.

[21] In this context, efficacious represents an approach that maximizes desired results (impact) and minimizes waste (inefficiency). While *effective* is an appropriate and often "effective" synonym, it is not sufficiently efficacious in this instance in that it does not encompass efficiency or achievement of a specific desired result (i.e., something can be wasteful and still be effective). The primary differentiator is that efficiency can lead to varying degrees of efficaciousness (or lack thereof).

Implementing Your Values Statements

Once your values statements have been written, leadership must commit to cultivating and ingraining them within the organization. Leaders must provide the tactical impetus behind adopting the company's values by acting as role models for everyone in the organization. The best way to start that process is with traditional change management and project management techniques.

The first step is to assign a sponsor from senior leadership to each value. The sponsor becomes the accountable party for demonstrating visible, tangible support. They are responsible for recruiting champions. The champions mentor and support managers, supervisors, and staff with the application of their assigned value to routine activities and decision-making responsibilities. Together, the sponsors and their champions become the vehicles for imbuing subconscious application of values throughout the company.

You want your values statements to be in everyone's mind as litmus tests for decisions and behavior. Encourage staff to share stories—as Britt's tech client did—of how values were applied in their work with others to see, hear, and for staff, to emulate. This is how organizational alignment and cultural strength are developed as you traverse the Arc of Success, grow, and add diversity.

It's not enough to have defined values that people know and intellectually embrace. Values need to do more to define behavior or culture. They must inform and guide planning and strategic efforts that lead to the future health of the organization. If the values and consistent examples of how they are applied are kept top of mind, decisions and behavior will become aligned as desired. It's an educational, entertaining, benign, and penalty-free form of cultural engineering.

Talking to a prospect, dealing with an unhappy customer, terminating an employee, conducting a meeting, simply knowing which option is best, and making difficult decisions all become second nature as stories guide and inform actions. The simple, mundane, even the complex repetitive tasks we routinely do were conscious acts before they became subconscious actions.

Snagging the full benefit of values statements demands a subconscious level of awareness—familiarity so intimate that thoughts and actions are consistently connected. Before they can become subconscious decisions and behaviors, they must be used consciously and proactively. Inculcating values is an activity that requires conscious thought when you begin and evolves into subconscious behavior with stunning celerity.

Maintaining Your Values Statements

As success brings growth, growth tends to dilute and corrode the culture you've worked so hard to create. Maintaining it can be built into routines as reminders delivered through story. Sharing stories makes your values come alive and creates a subtle enforcement mechanism that creeps into the mind when decisions are being made and actions are required. Stories become the instruction manual for the uninitiated and create virtual shared experiences.

Having a set of values for your business defines specific aspects of life while working. Stories that exemplify their use become instructional, entertaining, and part of your organizational lore, the definitive model for how staff are expected to act, even when nobody is watching. These stories become ingrained in the culture of your business and influence every thought, action, and decision made within it. Over time, your values will become part of the air every employee breathes and guide their behavior all day long.

Once properly implemented, the only maintenance required is when material change occurs. Typically driven by growth, you may need to add a value or create a different set of values for groups with proprietary operational demands uncommon to the rest of the organization.

One of the situations where revising values was appropriate was when a client's customer service department with five thousand employees was implementing a major change. The organization wanted to transform the problem-focused department's negative image as a cost center to a positive image that served as a competitive advantage and generated revenue. Knowing the culture of that department had to change for transformation to occur, the company's leaders began by creating a specific and separate set of values and values statements for their customer service department.

While rare, the need to remove a value can occur and should be done with good cause, transparency, and clear communication to all stakeholders.

Examples

A good values statement creates clarity and context about a specific individual value and how that value is interpreted and adopted. It is short enough to be remembered and simple enough to be easily read and spoken. Finally, a good values statement must be achievable. Unrealistic values-based expectations are worse than having nothing. In essence, a values statement that is unrealistic or unattainable says, "We don't care about values, but we pretend to have them because we have to. Truth is, we really couldn't care less."

One of the brick-and-mortar businesses I owned with a partner in the early 1990s, Square Tree Software, established seven values statements. The language was created with intent to help define our culture and sequenced by priority.

- We[22] are committed to *success*.
- We depend on *teamwork* (working together) to achieve shared goals.
- We are constantly *learning*.
- We value *honesty*.
- We operate with *integrity*.
- We embrace *change*.
- We always strive to have *fun*.

They served us well, and I continue to use them in my consulting practice.

---

[22] The use of *we* in my values statements represents the collaborative relationship between me, our clients, and our colleagues.

Value statements I like

- We hold ourselves *accountable* for what we set out to accomplish.

  This values statement is clear and would be difficult to misinterpret or twist into something it doesn't mean (i.e., that only they are accountable for what they set out to do). It is a perfect lead for telling a story about being accountable.

- Embrace *change.*

  This short statement overtly announces that the organization recognizes change is inevitable, that it will eagerly accept change, and that the organization will do its best to adopt the changes it faces in the most positive manner possible.

- We will maintain *strategic* and organizational *flexibility* to meet the challenges associated with the changing competitive landscape.

  The magic in this values statement is the combination of the strategic with the tactical. It recognizes short-term and long-term pressures and sets the tone for an organization that can adapt on the fly by being flexible.

- *Integrity* and *honesty.* Character counts. Reliability, trustworthiness, transparency. A commitment to fairness, honor, and truth.

  Integrity and honesty are common in values statements. I selected this as a positive example because it explains what integrity and honesty mean for this firm. While the statement does not define what the company considers fair, it does express a commitment to being fair. If fairness is the intent, the reason for doing something should be easily explainable and the perception of the act of fairness can be embraced or corrected. After all, nobody is perfect. When someone makes a mistake for the right reasons, it becomes a valuable, teachable lesson.

- *Teamwork.* A collaborative approach among lawyers and staff. Available, approachable, generous with one's time, sharing work, sending work to the right place in the firm. Cooperation.

Teamwork is often used when enthusiastic collaboration is what is intended. Teamwork can have negative connotations, particularly in larger organizations where it can easily be interpreted as... *"You do your work* and *my work."* That's not teamwork. This values statement digs into what teamwork really means in a tangible, tactical manner. There isn't much ambiguity in the meaning of what teamwork means to this firm or how to achieve it.

- *Fun.* We always strive to have fun.

Business is serious work, and what we do is important to ourselves and all our stakeholders from our families to our customers and communities. That doesn't mean we shouldn't enjoy our work. This value reminds us how important it is to look for the joy in all we do.

This value, striving to have fun, is one of my personal favorites, one I've used in all my businesses since the mid-1990s. Fun is always contextual. What some like, others may loathe. For example, when we had sales meetings, the salesperson being recognized had to stand on their chair and rise above everyone else standing in the room while being applauded—a stand ovation. For most of our programmers and engineers, that kind of recognition would have made them ill. They're typically quiet and avoid spotlights.

Other examples we used involved food on birthdays, having staff take turns at putting something completely off-topic into our monthly newsletter, and having contests to see who could come up with the best ideas as determined by different departments.

Value statements I don't like

- *Service.* Service encompasses the concept of quality in everything we do, having a service mindset when dealing with clients, and demanding a lot of ourselves.

  Service is an experience, not something you can put in a box and hand someone. There is no universal standard that defines good service. Most individuals have their own concept of what good service means and an intimate awareness when it isn't provided.

  An inexperienced customer may feel that a telephone support agent offering patient, detailed explanations and information is wonderful, while a more experienced customer may only be frustrated by that same experience.

  The inexperienced customer may feel lost with short, direct, to-the-point answers. Meanwhile, the experienced customer is likely to feel as if they're dragging an anchor trying to get that same short, direct, to-the-point answer that wasn't forthcoming from an employee new to the process.

  A "service" values statement requires greater clarity to eliminate confusion. How does a service mindset reveal itself in your business? To be effective, a value needs to help the employee understand what is expected of them and help the customer to have similar expectations.

- *Respect.* Respect for one another in the office will lead to greater productivity and staff satisfaction, which should result in lower turnover.

  The value, respect, can be incredibly positive when properly applied. Here, the texts that should be guiding situational behavior—*greater productivity* and *satisfaction* and *lower turnover*—describe objective measures of performance that have limited relevance to behavior and how respect is expressed. This statement is likely to do more harm than good.

- *Enthusiasm.* Enthusiasm is employing and nurturing staff with a passion for providing the highest-level quality service to our clients.

While the intent is laudable, the statement has several flaws. Enthusiasm can be positive for the right personality; to the apathetic, it can be quite negative. Using the phrase *highest-level quality* is unrealistic. Every client has their own individual perspective on what constitutes quality, and every business has boundaries, whether physical or policy-based.

Whenever a company talks about being the best, highest, leading, etc., it indicates lazy writing that highlights expectations that only one company can achieve (which is usually not the company making the claim). I have no issue with any organization striving to be the best, highest, leading, etc. I believe those aspirations are worthy of continuous pursuit, a never-ending journey, not a destination.

- We will require and reward excellence, teamwork, and strong client relationships.
- We will maintain an environment that requires integrity and teamwork and encourages creativity, a spirit of excitement, personal growth, and health.

Using the word *require* in a values statement implies each employee will be flogged, fined, or fired if they don't comply. *Require* is not a good word for a values statement, and this organization did it twice!

Reflecting on Values Statements

This chapter describes a new and different way to think about values statements for most leaders. To survive, businesses need to reinforce their abilities to thrive and grow. Whether your business needs to create, implement, or maintain values statements, the following questions will help reveal their potential and identify creative ways to apply and capitalize on this vital tool:

- How do you know staff understand your values and are guided by them the way intended?
- What are a few creative ways you can improve decision-making by actively using values statements? What about trust? What about recruiting or culture or any of the other benefits mentioned in this chapter?
- Does your business *have* values statements?
- Are they written, not in someone's head?
- Are they understood, embraced, and modeled by leadership and staff?
- How do you know?

Accessing and completing the Index scorecard survey is explained in chapter 12.

Key Points

Ch 1	Operational Imperatives	Clarity of purpose	Consistency of performance	Engagement of people
Ch 2	Stage of Maturity	Youth	Adolescence	Adulthood
Ch 2	Why leaders fail to achieve the 3 Ps	They didn't know they needed to do them.	They didn't know how to do them.	They forgot they needed to do them.
Ch 3	Arc of Success	New Ideas ► Growth ► Complexity ►Controls ► Less Flexibility		
Ch 3	Problems with Success	Symptoms masquerading as root problems	Historically good operational behaviors that begin to create undesirable results	Emotional resistance to beneficial change

Ch 3	Index Indicators & (chapter #)	**Values (4)** Vision (5) Mission (6)	Business Plan Marketing Plan Goals and Responsibilities	Systems and Structure Communications Plan

The values statements are one of the eight leading indicators of organizational success and sustainability. Leadership teams that care about long-term survival of their organizations should build and deploy all eight.

You should have three to seven business values statements.

Seven primary benefits of values statements are as follows:

- Company culture
- Trust
- Engagement
- Retention
- Marketing
- Recruiting
- Decision-making

CHAPTER 5

What You Want Your Business to Become: Vision Statement

Index Indicator #2

Business is a team sport. Winning requires coordinated group efforts and collective focus on common goals. Unlike sports, there are no championships and no competitions to anoint champions; business doesn't work that way.

At some point on the journey to success, every business has to decide what it wants to be when it grows up.

What do we want to accomplish?

What do we want to be known for in the future?

How will we plot a course to pursue those long-term dreams and eventually realize them?

Almost every leader I've known has asked themselves these questions at some point in their career.

The path forward for every business is fraught with myriad options and decisions to be made, each of which impacts the course of the organization—sometimes veering it away from its goals and dreams, sometimes nudging it back toward them. It's a maze with handfuls of right answers and bucketfuls of wrong and "maybe *this* will work" ones.

The first time I remember being exposed to the idea of a future-state vision was as a part of the Sacramento Metropolitan Chamber of Commerce leadership team. In addition to being on the board, I was also the cochair of the Small Business Training and Development Committee. As such, I was involved in numerous operational and strategic chamber activities, including annual planning.

In the early 1990s, the chamber assembled a group of staff and member-leaders to help define its future-state vision. We worked with a strategic planning facilitator to describe what the chamber would look like and be known for.

One group exercise was to create the front page of *The Sacramento Bee*, Sacramento's largest local paper, twenty years in the future. What were the stories being highlighted, and what role, if any, would the chamber have in them, good or bad? How did we want the community to see us in twenty years, and what would we need to do to find common ground and start working toward that shared, future-state vision?

That chamber visioning exercise was a sobering experience for me. We were being asked to decide the fate of the chamber, what we wanted it to be known for, the big-picture goals we wanted it to achieve, and how *we* were going to make them happen? The challenges of realizing our vision and the impact of succeeding were difficult to wrap my head around.

Businesses that endure over time and create a legacy have answers to these questions. Those answers, however lofty or improbable they may be, create emotional connections to the future state they describe which, in turn, creates energy and enthusiasm. When wielded wisely, a vision statement can have a unifying power while acting as the fertilizer that makes a business blossom and flourish.

For all these reasons, a vision statement is the most effective tool I've found for helping ensure a successful journey to wherever a business and its leaders choose to venture.

The Profit Monster

A successful business is about *much* more than profits. Profit *is* one of the many forms of measuring success and sustainability. The ability to generate revenues greater than costs to fund maintenance, operations, and development of new products and services is crucial for every business, including not-for-profits. When profit becomes the primary purpose, the thirst for more can become an insatiable soul-consuming monster.

The best way to battle the profit monster is with a vision of a tomorrow better than today. A vision for your business creates awareness of what must be done and begs for actions to achieve it while justifying the need for change. The vision of an organization should describe an audacious, yet realistic, and desirable future *yet to be attained.*

This concept of vision is one of the oldest human concepts. As evidence, and without endorsement or application to business, in Genesis, God gave Abraham and the Hebrews a vision of their promised land, commanded them to go there and make the world a better place.

As such, vision is one of the internally focused indicators in the Index. It should speak directly to staff and all internal stakeholders. A good vision statement will create the sense of a better place, a destination every member of the organization can emotionally embrace and contribute to achieving.

> *If you don't know where you are going, you'll end up someplace else.* (Yogi Berra)[23]

Benefits

Creating, documenting, and implementing a company vision statement has six primary benefits: strategy, foresight, collaboration, recruiting, business development, and psychological.

---

[23] Berra, Yogi. "Yogi Berra > Quotes > Quotable Quote," *Goodreads*. https://www.goodreads.com/quotes/23616-if-you-don-t-know-where-you-are-going-you-ll-end.

Strategy

Business strategy is a framework for actions designed to achieve long-term goals and desired results that move the organization closer to where leadership wants to take the company, i.e., the vision. Without a vision, long-term goals have no direction and desired results have nothing to move the business toward. Consequently, short-term nonstrategic goals are all that can be pursued.

Absent a vision, an organization is at liberty to drift in any direction like a boat without a keel, chasing fads and trends that eventually undermine dependability and stability, aspects of trust client's demand. Therefore, there can be no sustainability-enhancing strategy without a vision.

An organization without strategy cannot create or demonstrate a lasting value proposition to its customers or prospects or maintain long-term relationships with them. Clarity about what to do when change occurs can best be attained through the lens of a vision the organization continuously strives to achieve. Creating a vision statement facilitates long-term goals, provides a foundation of stability and dependability as by-products of clarity and focus, and through planning efforts, gives birth to foresight.

Foresight

The nature of vision as a window into a desired future forces leadership to look forward and anticipate next steps. This forward-looking mindset becomes second nature over time as the organization matures and begins to improve its ability to anticipate change, maintain pursuit of its vision, and adjust before unexpected change becomes disruptive and causes losses.

The better an organization becomes at developing foresight, the more effective it becomes at achieving interim desired results and moving closer to its vision. Foresight informs new strategies for continuous achievement of long- and short-term goals. Foresight feeds directly into stability and dependability as well as long-term relationships with staff and customers.

These enhanced relationships allow for mutually beneficial collaboration.

Collaboration

For healthy business teams, it's more fun to succeed with others than by yourself. Having a vision calls out to others who have similar desires, attracting them like metal to a magnet. The more aligned staff is toward achieving the vision, the better they'll be at working together to achieve it.

Collaboratively working with others toward a shared vision creates a natural route to individual satisfaction and organizational success. Creating a desirable, attractive environment leads to easier and more effective recruiting.

Recruiting

More customers and more staff are the two most common recruitment needs of most successful organizations. Any business overtly pursuing a comprehensible vision will naturally attract client and employee prospects who want to work with like-minded people and companies striving to realize their vision too.

When you share your vision in the hiring process and both you and your candidate agree to engage, the candidate will see themselves as self-selecting. These are the people you want to have on board. These are the people who will be as passionate about your vision as you are.

When passion for common needs and wants exists, many of the obstacles business development must overcome melt away.

Business development

When your company's vision is shared throughout its business development processes, it will be seen as forward-thinking and unwilling to rest on current successes. It will demonstrate pursuit of a better future and attract prospects it's best suited to serve. These are the customers who'll be proud to be doing business with you and sharing in your success. A vision-driven methodology is the most effective, least expensive catalyst to energize business development.

Easier and more effective business development feeds on itself as success accumulates and helps validate the goals and efforts of all involved. The accumulation of success has psychological benefits.

Psychological

As this book is focused on the impacts of change, perhaps one of the most valuable benefits of a vision statement is that it helps make change less destructive. By communicating the vision, you're creating awareness that change is being pursued and what that change will mean for everyone. When it happens, it won't be a surprise.

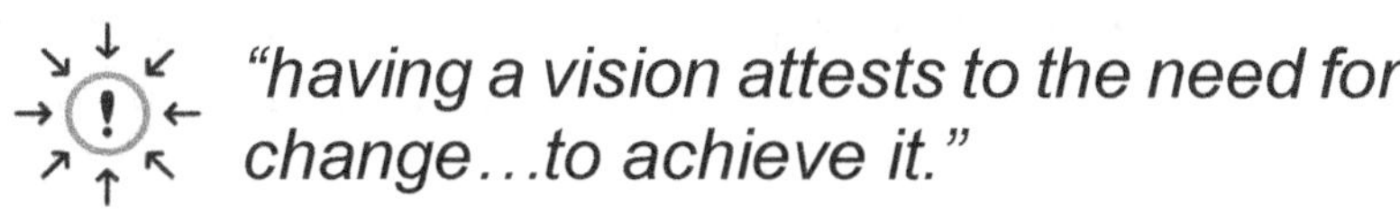

Having a vision attests to the need for change, preferably by design, to achieve it. As such, *your vision becomes the cornerstone in creating the desire to embrace change.*

Creating Your Vision Statement

While I've facilitated the creation of dozens of vision statements, I've yet to find a best practice for doing so. Each time I've helped a leadership team create their vision, regardless of their organization's maturity, it's been a different experience.

Typically, it takes months or years. Occasionally, leadership can be so closely aligned that the vision materializes out of a handful of words shuffled around on a sticky wall in a matter of minutes. One of my most enjoyable experiences took a leadership team of five less than two hours. When the statement suddenly appeared before us, the first person to speak said, "Kaboom," which was patiently and contemplatively followed by four separate, soft kabooms.

The vision statement must be clear and concise, creating a picture in everyone's mind of what the business will become if they execute their job with passion and skill. As the focal point of your business's success, the vision is often felt, even understood with crystal clear clarity by leadership while retaining an elusive quality that makes it difficult to document. Its connection to everything your business does tends to create a "greased pig" slipperiness when trying to capture it.

One way to begin is to gather the appropriate members of your organization in a quiet space where you won't be interrupted or distracted. Ask everyone to close their eyes and imagine themselves in the future, looking back at all the wonderful yet-to-be experiences you will have had while building and growing the business. When you're all in that mental place, ask yourselves these future-state questions and write down *everyone's* answers. Note: This is not an exhaustive list; it is offered as a starting point. I don't have the perfect questions for *you*.

- Where are you?
- What are you doing?
- What are others doing around you?
- What products or services are offered?
- What problems do they solve?
- What value do they add?
- Who benefits?
- Now that cash flow is not an issue, what does the business have that it couldn't afford in prior years?
- What makes you most proud to be associated with the organization?

After capturing everyone's answers, take some time to absorb and digest them. Look for comments that represent your wants, desires, how you feel about your organization. Be patient; this takes time. When you find things that connect, write them down on a separate sheet of paper. Gather everyone's papers, eliminate duplicates, group them in ways that feel good, and start shuffling them into sentences.

This is where time can be your enemy. It seems, the more you struggle, the harder it will be to find answers. Everyone needs to be relaxed and clearheaded. Take the time to think, talk, and ponder. It should take several hours and sessions, weeks, and maybe even years. As I said earlier, creating a good vision statement takes time. One very successful business owner I knew took almost seven years to find his. When he found and implemented it, his business exploded, growing a hundredfold in just over one year.

Technology has stimulated dynamics that can create uncommon weaknesses in your vision statement. One example is described by Lawrence Gregory from the Panmore Institute (http://panmore.com) as it applies to Amazon's vision statement, which is listed below under examples.

"Amazon.com's vision statement possesses strong characteristics, such as the specification of the company's target market and an aspect of its marketing mix. However, this corporate vision satisfies only some of the conventional characteristics of ideal vision statements. For example, Amazon's corporate vision is concise, clear, and abstract enough to ensure suitability in various areas of the business. Still, this corporate vision is not stable enough to ensure its suitability in the future of the business. For instance, Amazon's business now includes cloud services and brick-and-mortar bookstores. Yet, the company's vision statement still focuses on e-commerce."[24]

When you find that special cluster of words that makes you say "Kaboom!" or even "Ooh, I like that!", be deliberate, be patient, and live with it for a bit. Take it for a cross-country test-drive. Run it by staff, clients, vendors, friends, and family. Check in with each group of stakeholders and make time to process what they tell you.[25] Build confidence your business will be able to live with the vision for the rest of its life.

---

[24] "Amazon.com Inc.'s Mission Statement & Vision Statement (An Analysis)," Panmore Institute, 13 February 2019, http://panmore.com/ amazon-com-inc-vision-statement-mission-statement-analysis.

[25] This activity often stimulates business development opportunities.

Implementing Your Vision Statement

The tactical value of a vision statement is in the target it provides. If strategy helps achieve a predetermined goal or reach a desirable destination, a strategic objective helps move you closer to that goal.

The first step in implementation is to develop strategic objectives that move the business closer to the vision. Yes, it's the old, tired, worn, *and effective* strategic planning effort.

Your vision validates you're headed in the right direction and toward your ultimate end goals. When you encounter obstacles, adjust your path. Sometimes you'll need to carve new paths that haven't existed before.

When you have a vision and strategy to get you there, you'll know when you're off course. Whether due to poor planning, execution, or a change in your environment, your vision helps ensure progress toward an end goal as you go through the trials and tribulations of growth and maturation.

Maintaining Your Vision

When you've succeeded and captured your business's vision statement, it should be lasting, the one business element that shouldn't need to change. The only indispensable component of maintenance involves aliveness.

For your vision to have life, it must be actively pursued and milestones celebrated. Strategic objectives are the vehicles that will carry your business to its vision. Every year you should review them and reflect on any progress made toward the vision. Strategic objectives fall into one of three categories:

- We succeeded. What's next? Make new ones.
- We're making progress. What are our obstacles? Keep your vision alive by proactively examining any obstacles and adjust strategies to reinforce active pursuit of your vision.
- We were wrong. What now? Take a step back and rethink your strategies.

Active pursuit of strategic objectives moves you closer to the vision inch by inch. Regularly scheduled review and reflection of them by your leadership team will ensure the business is still on target and allows for course correction when change happens. It also provides fuel for staying top of mind while creating opportunities to celebrate progress and achievements.

Risk Alert: Successful achievement of any strategic objective tends to diminish any sense of immediacy to replace it with a new one. Your business should *always* be actively pursuing at least one short-term, one near-term, and one long-term strategic objective. When you complete one, a strategy session should be quickly convened to replace it.

My vision statement continues to be a work in progress: To change the way businesses do business so that everyone who wants a job has one they enjoy, and employers enjoy and value their staff.

Examples

Vision Statements I Like

River Garden Farms

"The 21st century model for sustainable farming in harmony with the environment, River Garden Farms has become an example of courage, leadership, and social responsibility. Through generations, River Garden Farms continues to thrive."[26]

I like this example because the idea of becoming a model creates a sense of broad acceptance and reach. Coupling model with the twenty-first century creates a futuristic viewpoint looking back at a century of recognized success. It sounds big, it feels big, and it certainly is a bit audacious—a big, hairy, audacious goal (BHAG).

---

[26] River Garden Farms, Knights Landing, CA.

The River Garden Farms vision statement says what the company does, "sustainable farming in harmony with the environment," in generic yet meaningful terms without using the overused and commonly misleading organic label. Finally, it closes with a nod to success and sustainability: "Continues to thrive…through generations."

California Institute for Behavioral Health Solutions

"The California Institute for Behavioral Health Solutions (CIBHS) is the recognized leader in developing world-class behavioral health programs and systems."[27]

I like this example because it's active—developing world-class behavioral health programs and systems—and implies past, present, and future value. Being world-class implies global competitiveness in an environment with global reach, mental health.

Being a recognized leader is the only aspect I would like to see a bit stronger with clarity about who will be recognizing them. The scope and proactive aspects of the CIBHS vision statement qualify it as another BHAG.

Amazon

"To be earth's most customer-centric company; to build a place where people can come to find and discover anything they might want to buy online."[28]

I love this example because it demonstrates the good and exposes two subtle weaknesses of a company vision for a company most humans buy from. The Amazon vision statement includes two extremely aspirational and powerful ideas—find and discover anything they might want—that work well in a vision statement.

---

[27] "What We're About, About," CIBHS, California Institute for Behavioral Health Solutions, 2015, https://www.cibhs.org/what-were-about.

[28] "Amazon Mission and Vision Statement Analysis," MissionStatement.com, Mission Statement Academy, 19 June 2019, https://mission-statement.com/amazon/.

The weaknesses are found in the close, "to buy online." The term *online* is modern and seems clear in today's world even though it has not proven durable over time. Who's to say the internet will be referred to as the online marketplace for years, decades, or longer? Who's to say the internet won't be replaced by some other form of technological connectedness? It leaves open the possibility of becoming perishable and obsolete. And as previously stated in the review by Panmore above, many of Amazon's most lucrative revenue streams are not from people buying online. In this way, Amazon's vision statement is limiting and exposes another durability weakness.

Vision Statements I Don't Like

The University of Illinois Springfield

"The University of Illinois Springfield will be a pathway to opportunity, a catalyst for change and a space of possibility where learners become ethical and passionate scholars, leaders and citizens capable of transforming their local and global communities."[29]

This vision statement demonstrates an awkwardness that undermines current strengths by stating "will be a pathway" and "where learners become" as if they don't exist today and will be realized in the future. If the university *will be* a pathway to opportunity and where learners *become* ethical and passionate scholars, then *it isn't those things yet*. This makes the University of Illinois at Springfield sound like an educational institution I wouldn't want to spend tens or hundreds of thousands of dollars on for the education of me or my children.

---

[29] "Mission, Vision, Values", Strategic Compass, University of Illinois at Springfield, The Office of Web Services, 2021, https://www.uis.edu/strategiccompass/mission-vision-values/.

Etsy

"Building an Etsy Economy."[30]

I have two problems with Etsy's vision statement. It says the company wants to "build an…economy," which is something only governments can do, making their vision unrealistic, unattainable, and not particularly inspirational or aspirational to me. The other reason is that it describes building something, which, even if they could, would mean there would be no reason for them to exist after they finished. While that may sound like circular logic, I think it's embarrassing.

Warby Parker

"We believe that buying glasses should be easy and fun. It should leave you happy and good-looking, with money in your pocket. We also believe that everyone has the right to see."

This vision statement is about belief in two values: easy and fun, not a vision. It talks about what an experience should feel like, not what they're going to become as an organization. That's not a bad thing, and it doesn't belong in a vision statement.

If you review the benefits of a good vision statement with an internally focused perspective, Warby Parker's eliminates the last four of them: collaboration, recruiting, business development, and psychological. Additional problems include my distaste for overt comments about other people's money: "with money in your pocket." It makes me want to ask how much and implies they're going to take control of my money. And since when did vision become a right? It may never be converted into braille, and blind people may never hear or read it. I still find the vision somewhat insulting. They could have easily said quality improvement to their vision with quality eyeglasses.

---

[30] Stockton, Blake. "17 Vision Statement Examples to Spark Your Imagination", vision-statement-examples, Fit Small Business, 18 September 2020, https:// fitsmallbusiness.com/vision-statement-examples/.

Reflecting on Vision Statements

This chapter describes a new and different way to think about a vision statement for most leaders. To survive, businesses need to reinforce their abilities to thrive and grow. Whether your business needs to create, implement, or maintain a vision statement, the following questions will help reveal their potential and identify clever ways to apply and capitalize on this vital tool:

- How do you get staff buy-in to long-term goals?
- Does your vision statement guide operations?
- What are a few creative ways you can improve tolerance for change by actively using a vision statement? What about collaboration? What about strategy or foresight or any of the other benefits mentioned in this chapter?
- Does your organization *have* a vision statement?
- Is it documented, not in someone's head?
- Is it understood, embraced, and modeled by leadership and staff?
- How do you know?

Accessing and completing the Index scorecard survey is explained in chapter 12.

Key Points

Ch 1	Operational Imperatives	Clarity of purpose	Consistency of performance	Engagement of people
Ch 2	Stage of Maturity	Youth	Adolescence	Adulthood
Ch 2	Why leaders fail to achieve the 3 Ps	They didn't know they needed to do them.	They didn't know how to do them.	They forgot they needed to do them.
Ch 3	Arc of Success	New Ideas ► Growth ► Complexity ►Controls ► Less Flexibility		
Ch 3	Problems with Success	Symptoms masquerading as root problems	Historically good operational behaviors that begin to create undesirable results	Emotional resistance to beneficial change
Ch 3	Index Indicators & (chapter #)	Values (4) **Vision (5)** Mission (6)	Business Plan Marketing Plan Goals and Responsibilities	Systems and Structure Communications Plan

The vision statement is the second of eight leading index indicators of organizational success and sustainability.

Business is a team sport. The best teams yearn for guidance, motivation, and a shared purpose.

A business is more than a pursuit of profit.

A vision statement is critical to long-term success, and they typically take a long time to create. Years are not uncommon.

Your vision statement should focus internally on staff who drive the organization, create pride in the journey, and describe a valuable destination everyone can see in their mind's eye. It should also support, not undermine, the major benefits of a vision statement.

Six primary benefits of a vision statement are as follows:

- Strategy
- Foresight
- Collaboration
- Recruiting
- Business development
- Psychological

CHAPTER 6

The Value Your Business Delivers: Mission Statement

Index Indicator #3

A mission statement should focus externally on the people and businesses that benefit from the products and services your business provides. A good mission statement has three clearly described elements:

1. The market being served
2. The value being delivered
3. How that value is delivered to that market

One of the more effective ways to think about your mission is as the answer to the question "What's in it for the customer?"[31]

Does it matter whether an organization has a mission statement? Does it matter whether staff memorize it? How much of a difference can a mission statement make? A mission statement won't solve cash flow problems, employee problems, or more-work-than-we-can-handle problems—or could it?

In my experience, very few leaders truly understand the power of a mission statement, much less what makes a mission statement work. In fact, the concept of mission statements has been so bastard-

---

[31] The mission statement and marketing plans are the only two externally focused Index indicators. The other six are designed around the distinctiveness of the business.

ized that the terms *mission statement, vision statement,* and *purpose statement* have become synonymous and uniformly misapplied in what seems to be a majority of businesses.

I routinely observe people rolling their eyes when someone starts talking about mission statements. The opinion held by too many is that they're worthless, and they're right. A half-assed, poorly written, poorly deployed mission statement is worthless.

The concept of a mission statement may be elusive, but it's not compelling until you feel the exhilaration that comes from channeling the enthusiasm that launched the business. A statement that energizes when embraced and employed creates visible, measurable, tangible results. One example comes from Innovative Education Management Inc., which is in the "Mission Statements I Like" section below.

The mission statement is the third and last Index indicator for creating clarity of purpose.

Benefits

The benefits of a well-conceived, well-written, and properly utilized mission statement are huge and permeate most operational aspects of an organization. Some of the most tangible, moving, and quantifiable are condensed below.

Creating, documenting, and implementing a company mission statement has six primary benefits: financial, psychological, productivity, quality, durability, and recruiting.

Financial (another bone for the numbers and finance people)

Time and money are two of the most valuable resources a business has. If squandered, they can't be reclaimed. When value delivered is clear and the allure of an inappropriate or glamour sale opportunity presents itself, the mission helps take emotion out of the decision to pursue or ignore. Prospects outside your target market aren't likely to do business with you or be profitable, long-term customers. They often become toxic.

Avoiding prospects outside your sweet spot squanders time and money spent chasing them. Because they're not your target market, they're also unlikely to be comfortable doing business with you. Your mission should be a gatekeeper in your pursuit of prospects and projects. Reducing unnecessary overhead allows staff to focus on the things that create value, which leads me to more profit and the next benefit.

Psychological

The mission statement is the starting point for communicating what you do and why people want to do business with you. When buyers know what to expect, their expectations are aligned with your intentions. Saying what you do and doing what you say make most people happy.

Providing customers with things they want and need makes them feel good. Appreciative customers fuel organizations, and staff feel valued. A sense of value, whether delivered or received, improves morale and makes an organization a more desirable place to work and do business with. Oh yeah, and it makes customers want to buy more, aka sustainable profitability. See financial above.

Productivity

The joy of doing and being appreciated are the stimulants of productivity. An insightful parable commonly attributed to Confucius reads, "Choose a job you love, and you will never have to work a day in your life." When people enjoy their work, they take pride in what they do. As described in the Arc of Success, when something is successful, human nature drives most people to do more of it.

Happy staff doing more work and enjoying themselves is a form of productivity. True productivity cannot exist without quality.

Quality

The nature of productivity is doing more and doing better. The better aspect of this equation is where quality comes into play. Think about quality in terms of getting what you think you're paying for. When expectations are unfulfilled, quality becomes the scapegoat.

A clear statement of the value your organization delivers and whom it's delivering to provides the opportunity to refine and improve all aspects of client interactions. From internal operations to problem-solving after the sales, profitable companies with confident staff, customers, and vendors are more productive and do better work. People are attracted to the positive energy these organizations exude. They become magnets for profit, and quality is their byproduct.

Durability[32]

Properly implementing the three elements of a good mission statement conveys a sense of commitment. Publicly stating whom you serve, how you serve them, and the value you deliver gives audiences confidence you'll do what you say *and be around to keep doing so*. Using your mission statement as a compass for staff while pursuing their goals and responsibilities creates consistency when options exist, or the path forward isn't clear.

When staff, customers, vendors, and the communities they operate within are aligned around the value your business delivers, pressure to change transforms into gratitude for stability and reinforces durability. The consistency and emotions that can be generated with a mission statement, commitment, confidence, and gratitude create a desirable place to work, a company people want to do business with, and a magnet for recruitment.

Recruitment

As stated in chapter 5, more customers and more staff are the two most common recruitment needs for any successful organization.

---

[32] "Able to Resist Wear, Decay, etc., Well; Lasting; Enduring." Durability. 2018. In dictionary.com. Retrieved September 27, 2018, from https://www.dictionary.com/browse/durability?s=t.

Everybody wants more customers. Incorporating your mission statement into your sales process has two customer-recruitment benefits. Customers know when the value you offer is something they care about and might be willing to buy. And it helps the organization avoid getting sucked into business opportunities that can be disruptive, costly, even harmful in some cases.

The need for more staff lives in the pursuit of growth. Two benefits materialize when you incorporate your mission statement into your staff recruitment process. Candidates can choose your organization more confidently knowing they will be doing something they care about with like-minded people. Those candidates are most likely to be connected to and passionate about your mission.

The President's Anecdote
The New Consultant

It was the first time the not-for-profits leadership team had met with me, the new consultant hired to solve some of their bigger, strategic problems. Collectively, they were responsible for an eight-figure budget and a couple of hundred staff with a fiduciary obligation to the community funding them. I was confronted with eight people staring at me with frowns, blank faces, gratuitous smiles, and acting as if they didn't know what to think or how to react.

"Do you have a mission statement?" I asked.

It wasn't hard to read my audience. The expressions on their faces were full of frustration.

The CFO's face said, "Mission statement? We're having cash flow problems, and he's asking about our mission statement!"

The CMO's face said, "Mission statement? We're having trouble just finding the time to take care of our current clients, much less look for new ones, and he's asking about our mission statement!"

The COO's face said, "Mission statement? We're having trouble getting our staff to do their jobs, and he's asking about our mission statement!"

The PMO chiefs' face said, "Mission statement? We need *help*, and he's asking about our mission statement!"

"Mission statement?" I repeated.

I heard mumbling.

Some words sounded like yes. Two heads nodded with less than full-throated confidence, and the faces of the other three went blank.

Bodies shifted in their seats as smartphones and tablets were called to action searching for their elusive mission statement.

"It has something to do with satisfied clients, happy employees. There's something in there about service and support," said the CMO.

"I think it says something about timeliness, or maybe it's responsiveness," said the PMO chief.

"It's on the website," murmured the COO, an original member of the start-up team. "I'm looking it up now."

The CFO's expression was an open-faced sandwich filled with disgust and a few sour pickles that read, "And we're actually paying for this…"

With a slightly defensive tone, the president said, "It was written by the board. We aren't that connected to it, but they really liked it and wanted us to adopt it, so we did."

"Okay, then, let me ask." I began, "How are you managing your sales team? Who are they supposed to be selling to? On what are their quotas and commissions based?"

Stares. Silence. Looking back and forth at one another, struggling to respond, opening and closing their mouths like fish out of water. Each wearing expressions of hope that someone else would respond.

Yet there were no answers.

Creating Your Mission Statement

The mission statement is a tool. Clients routinely ask if theirs is right or wrong. I find the question misguided. What you create and how you use it makes it effective, useless, or problematic.

An effective mission statement accurately communicates the value your organization delivers to its clients and helps grow your business. When properly implemented and maintained, a mission statement will also recruit and secure loyal customers, improve the structure and operations of your business, and keep your employees informed of their purpose and responsibilities while improving company morale. Creating a useless or problematic mission statement can be a tremendous waste of time and effort.

Now that I've highlighted the value and importance of a good mission statement, it's time to create yours and actualize those benefits for your company. Doing so is curiously simple but not so easy.

Simple to create because the pieces are specific. Not so easy to create because the most effective statements require the language of your customers. Simple to achieve the benefits because there are only four clear principles[33] to abide by. Not so easy to achieve because stepping a bit outside your comfort zone and embracing some change will be necessary.

The mission statement is the tactical component of purpose. Outwardly facing, it tells your target market why they should do business with you. It should be designed with your prospects in mind and written in their language. Your mission statement will have value internally when used as noted above in psychological and recruiting benefits. Think of it as the organization's promise to every customer. Use it to guide sales efforts and maintain focus on delivering value to the right customers.

An organization without a meaningful mission statement simply cannot use its resources[34] wisely or operate efficiently; it cannot create sustainable growth.

To ensure common understanding when shared with others without modification or inaccurate interpretations, you need it to be in writing.

The first step in creating your mission statement is to identify the people best able to share your markets' perception of your value. Reach out to a cross section of your clients and vendors. Be sure to

---

[33] If you made it this far without reading the introduction or forget them, you can refer to them on page 16.

[34] Every organization has three primary resources: human capital, time, and money. *Human capital* is a loose term that refers to knowledge, experience, and skills of an employee.

include those familiar with a broad range of your products and services. Include customers who like you as well as those who have issues with you. The negative perceptions are often the most valuable.

You must be nonthreatening, transparent, and avoid any appearance of a marketing or sales effort. Be open about what you're trying to accomplish and how the data being gathered will be used. Remember, you're asking them to help you make your business better. Your focus at this point is to identify the words they use, not get them to buy more from you. The ideal approach is to use an independent third party, and the goal is to capture the words your customers use to describe your value to them.

Some sample questions that might help include the following:

- What triggers you to contact us?
- What are the emotions you feel before, during, and after you engage with us?
- What are the things you hope will happen when you work with us?
- What are the things you are worried about when you work with us?
- Who would you contact if we weren't able to serve your needs?

Once you have collected customer feedback, assemble a cross section of staff and begin extracting words and phrases that describe the three components of your mission statement. Be playful, be purposeful.

The easiest way to get buy-in for any business activity is to involve those affected by it in its design and implementation. Therefore, it's critical to have leadership, management, and staff involved in the creation (or revision) and implementation of your mission statement. Depending on the size and diversity of your business, a mission statement can be of sufficient value for departments to create their own mission "nested" within the company's.

<u>Risk Alert</u>: If you have a board of directors, they should not be involved in this process. As stated above, the mission statement

describes the tactics that will lead to the achievement of strategic objectives. The board is strategic and should avoid getting involved in the tactical aspects of the organization.

Implementing Your Mission Statement

Once your mission statement has been written, leadership must be committed to it. They will be the driving force behind its success and must act as role models for everyone in the organization. To elevate its importance and the company's dedication to living up to it, your mission statement needs to be seen, heard, and lived throughout the business.

It should be on everything public. Whenever you communicate, your mission should be part of your outreach. Put it on your invoices, statements, signage, business cards, showroom, and all advertising. When communicating with prospects, the relevant aspects of your mission for them should be highlighted in all their messaging.

Your mission should be your company's mantra—open specific internal business meetings with it. Put it in your reception area, hallways, offices, break, and recreational areas. Some companies even put it in their restrooms. Everyone needs to live it.

You want it to be omnipresent, integrated into the ongoing daily operations of your organization. It should be repeated as often as possible to reinforce its importance and work its magic. Frequent repetition reminds everyone of who your customers are, the value they are paying for, and your dedication to delivering it.

Maintaining Your Mission

A mission statement should not be carved in stone. A successful organization is growing, and growth can involve new markets, products, services, and customer benefits. Growth can also require reorganizing the company to accommodate change and maintain efficiency, productivity, and quality. When do you need to revise your mission statement? Two external realities determine its life span:

1. When the products and services you provide to the market(s) you serve cease to be profitable, what you do and/or whom you do it for needs to change.
2. When your organization changes, your mission statement may be misaligned with the markets you serve, the value you deliver, or the manner in which you deliver it. See comments re: Amazon's mission statement above.

You *need* to revise your mission statement when something changes and it's no longer accurate or relevant.

The mission statement is the third leading index indicator of organizational success and sustainability. Start the journey now toward clarity of purpose. Make the commitment to bring your mission statement to life and secure unexpected dividends for years to come. You're beginning anew; enjoy the rush of liftoff.

Examples

A good mission statement is easy to remember and repeat. As Enron teaches us, a good mission statement is also accurate.

Mission Statements I Like

Innovative Education mission statement

"We believe in honoring individual education choices. We commit to providing an innovative public education environment for students, their parents, and teachers by empowering them to create learning opportunities which develop responsible and contributing members of society."

This organization is clear about whom they serve and the value they provide. This statement is not catchy or short, so it's not easy to remember or repeat. Because their message seems to resonate so powerfully to such a large segment of society, parents and their kids, the importance of being concise or memorable is reduced.

Red Cross

"The American Red Cross prevents and alleviates human suffering in the face of emergencies by mobilizing the power of volunteers and the generosity of donors."[35]

I like this mission statement because of its aspirational nature, something usually applied to vision statements, Here, human suffering is the target, not a specific demographic. Their value is clear—prevent and alleviate…suffering—without trying to apply objective measures to it, another aspirational element with no boundaries or criteria which I find powerful and refreshing.

Regarding the how, volunteers and donors are people like you and me. Most of us volunteer and donate, which creates an immediate connection and empathy for them in their mission. After all, if they do something we do too, it has to be right, doesn't it?

Finally, it's short enough and compelling enough to be memorized and repeated. It's clean and easy to say out loud, and it's a mission everyone who associates with them can be proud of.

"I'm not satisfied with the new mission statement. I can still understand parts of it."[36]

Mission Statements I Don't Like

Albertsons

"To create a shopping experience that pleases our customers; a workplace that creates opportunities and a great working envi-

---

[35] Red Cross, "Mission and Values," American Red Cross, https://www.redcross.org/about-us/who-we-are/mission-and-values.html.

[36] © Glasbergen. Reproduced with permission of Glasbergen Cartoon Service.

ronment for our associates; and a business that achieves financial success."[37]

In November of 2013, Albertsons' online mission statement earned them a spot in Inc.com's list of the nine worst mission statements of all time. To Albertsons' credit, it was later removed. Even though it was a short-lived effort that failed, it does serve as a good example of a bad mission statement.

Focusing first on the three elements of a good mission statement, this one does not describe the market being served, the value being delivered, or the manner of its delivery. I don't consider a pleasing shopping experience to be a value people should have to pay for. It's also not particularly easy to remember or repeat.

Perhaps the most egregious aspect of this mission statement is it focuses internally on the company; financial success and 'opportunities and a great working environment for our associates'—something I'd prefer to hear from the associates. If all you had was their mission, you'd have no idea what kind of business this is or the products or services they sell. What's clear is there are shopping opportunities and they want to make money.

Kickstarter

"Our mission is to help bring creative projects to life."[38]
I'm confident every project on the Kickstarter site was proposed by someone who felt their idea was creative. Unfortunately, that speaks to one component of their marketplace. Without investors, those projects represent energy and effort producing eye candy and experience.

I have no doubt as to Kickstarter value. My issue is with their poor attempt to capture their mission. As I see it, the most fundamental aspect of what they do is connect investors with creators/

---

[37] Zetlin, M. (2013, November 15), "The 9 Worst Mission Statements of All Time." Retrieved from https://www.inc.com/minda-zetlin/9-worst-mission-statements-all-time.html.

[38] "About," Kickstarter, https://www.kickstarter.com/about.

entrepreneurs. The act of making connections is what social media and the internet are all about. How could they miss that?

Reflecting on the Mission Statement

This chapter describes a new and different way to think about a mission for most leaders. To survive, businesses need to reinforce their abilities to thrive and grow. Whether your business needs to create, implement, or maintain its mission statement, the following questions will help reveal their potential and identify clever ways to apply and capitalize on this vital tool:

- If you asked every employee what value your business provides, would they all have the same answer? Would your customers?
- What are a few creative ways you can improve productivity by actively using a mission statement? What about profitability? What about quality or recruiting or any of the other benefits mentioned in this chapter?
- Does your organization *have* a mission statement?
- Is it documented, not in someone's head?
- Is it understood, embraced, and modeled by leadership and staff?
- How do you know?

Accessing and completing the Index scorecard survey is explained in chapter 12.

Key Points

Ch 1	Operational Imperatives	Clarity of purpose	Consistency of performance	Engagement of people
Ch 2	Stage of Maturity	Youth	Adolescence	Adulthood
Ch 2	Why leaders fail to achieve the 3 Ps	They didn't know they needed to do them.	They didn't know how to do them.	They forgot they needed to do them.
Ch 3	Arc of Success	New Ideas ► Growth ► Complexity ►Controls ► Less Flexibility		
Ch 3	Problems with Success	Symptoms masquerading as root problems	Historically good operational behaviors that begin to create undesirable results	Emotional resistance to beneficial change
Ch 3	Index Indicators & (chapter #)	Values (4) Vision (5) **Mission (6)**	Business Plan (7) Marketing Plan (8) Goals & Responsibilities (9)	Systems & Structure (10) Communications Plan (11)

The mission statement should focus externally on the people and businesses that benefit from the products and services your business provides. A good mission statement has three clearly described elements:

1. The market being served
2. The value being delivered
3. How that value is delivered to that market

Six primary benefits of mission statements are as follows:

- Financial
- Psychological
- Productivity
- Quality
- Durability
- Recruiting

PART 3

ADOLESCENCE AND THE SECOND P: CONSISTENCY OF PERFORMANCE

The pursuit of consistent performance in an ever-changing business environment has its own ironic conflict. The resolution to the conflict is achieved by focusing on consistency in commitments to clients, colleagues, and vendors. Then the tactical aspects of individual and organizational performance need to be nimble enough to ensure those commitments are consistently met.

Consistency comes from repetition, familiarity, and limiting change, unexpected occurrences, or conformity, which defines what is acceptable and what isn't, an inherently limiting dynamic.

Once your business has identified, accepted, and embraced its purpose, the need for growth becomes secondary to the need for consistency and quality achieved through restrictive guidelines and boundaries. The irony? The way growth is achieved becomes more important than the growth itself.

An inability to deliver consistent performance is the primary cause of business failure in the second stage of maturity, adolescence. Three fundamental indicators define performance: business plans, marketing plans, and goals and responsibilities (G&R). These three are the operational must-haves for continued organizational growth, or sustainability, and success.

CHAPTER 7

Strategies and Tactics: Business Plan

Index Indicator #4

Your business plan is a roadmap and decision-making tool. As a tool, it will help identify goals for the coming period, typically one year, and goals from the prior period to refresh and continue pursuing. Consider those pursuits as taking your business on a journey to a future destination. As a roadmap, the plan will help document actions for achieving goals, resources required to do so, and milestones to measure your progress.

Your organization needs to work as a team to achieve these goals. By thinking of your business plan as a roadmap with clear milestones, everyone will understand where you want them to go and when they get there. As with any journey, some preparation is essential. If staff can't read your mind, they won't know which route to take or how to adjust to unplanned detours.

Without a shared business plan, everyone will have to fill in the blanks themselves. Left to their own devices, they will unintentionally create chaos out of whatever order you think you've established, taking your business off in directions you didn't want to go and fighting with one another about how to get there.

Benefits

Providing your fellow travelers with a road map will help ensure no one gets lost along the way. By having a written business plan, or road map as many prefer to call it, everyone can feel secure, confident they're working toward the same goals.

Creating, documenting, and implementing a business plan has seven primary benefits: foresight, engagement, alignment of staff, planning, communication, resources, and financial.

Foresight

One of your business plan's most important benefits is minimizing the need to react. Having a well-thought-out plan and executing it reduces the likelihood of unexpected occurrences. It helps you and your staff be prepared and think things through. By proactively determining the path your business will follow, you'll be less likely to be distracted and better prepared to accommodate unexpected change while maintaining continuity and profitability.

Engagement

Most people want to do a good job in their work and don't like to be blindsided with surprises or unexpected demands. When properly created and implemented, a business plan helps eliminate assumptions and unknowns staff might worry about even though they haven't happened. It gives them specifics to focus on and provides a sense of contribution to the overall success of the company. Engagement is the natural by-product of staff contributions.

Alignment of staff

The business plan helps everyone understand the business plans and activities for the coming year. Awareness of the big picture creates a window for individuals to identify opportunities management may not recognize, opportunities for creating efficiencies, economies of scale, and new ideas that could be your next competitive advantage or major source of revenue.

Planning

Creating a business plan facilitates the identification of your organization's operational needs for the coming year[39] and allows staff to prepare to fulfill them. Effective planning cannot be done while executing. The business plan allows each process to receive the attention it needs and deserves.

Thinking through the needs in advance and documenting them helps everyone identify and understand activities that are the most important and time-sensitive. It also helps remove emotional "wants" and pressure that accompanies the tyranny of the urgent.

Communication

A business plan creates a shared understanding of near-term objectives your team is supposed to be working toward and how to achieve them. Unlike the childhood game of "Pass the Story," also known as "telephone," it can deliver a consistent message to a broad group of people when needed or convenient for them to receive it. Your business plan also provides a common point of reference around which your team can collaborate to use their collective wisdom and create greater value.

Resources

If the resources of a business can be described in three words, I believe they are *people*, *time*, and *money*—assets that cannot be replaced when squandered. When used properly, these assets lead to maximization of ROI. When your goals and objectives have been

---

[39] The period of time, or duration, for a business plan should vary based on the cycles of the organization it's designed for. Most organizations operate on an annual cycle. If yours is one that doesn't, your planning cycle should mirror your most dominant operational cycle.

defined and the actions to achieve them have been made clear, the likelihood of productive use of resources increases and the opportunities for waste become less appealing.

Financial

Documenting the details of the coming year's activities allows for planning the financial aspects of resource consumption and creating milestones for monitoring progress. Emotional debate over unplanned wants can be minimized or eliminated. Pursuit of objectives that fail can be easily identified and adjustments confidently made. These *course corrections* can result in substantial savings of effort (people), time, and money.

Daniel's Anecdote
The Annual Planning Session

It was the first Wednesday in November and Jewel Distribution's senior staff were assembled for their weekly management meeting. This Wednesday was one of those spectacular East Coast fall mornings where the sky was clear, the sun was bright, and the air was crisp—the kind of morning that almost makes waking up and going to work fun. But not this morning. Today was "Planning Day."

Every year Daniel gathered his leadership team to work on next year's road map, what most people call a business plan. Planning Day is a lot like the "Block of Cheese Day" episode from the *West Wing* TV series. The fictional chief of staff, Leo McGary, calls his senior staff in to give them his annual speech about listening to the people who have no voice, the people commonly thought of as "on the fringe."

Most of McGarry's team grumble and complain. By the end of the day, compassion and new insights have changed attitudes. Jewel's senior staff seem to follow that TV script meticulously, with the same people grumbling about the same things year after year. This year, Andy, the firm's lead developer, was conspicuously absent when their sales manager, Chip Jones, lobbed the first grenade.

"Seriously, I know I've said this many times before, but is all this time spent planning really necessary? I just don't see how this is going to help my team make any more sales or be more profitable. What's worse, it makes them feel like management doesn't trust them or think they're competent."

"Chip, let's not get carried away," Daniel responded. "We've been having these Planning Days for years, and when we're done, the entire team has always agreed, they are valuable. Over the years, I've received a lot of feedback from your staff about how much the insights and adjustments to how we approach our markets have helped them be more successful in getting new clients and growing their existing ones."

Some grumbled because they didn't like the process; others grumbled because they didn't like the complaints. Others were eager to dive in and get started.

Daniel continued, "So I assume everyone has reread last year's road map, yes?"

Everyone nodded in agreement.

"Okay then, you all know how this works, and we all know our vision and mission statements. What do we want to accomplish this year that will help move us closer to our vision? How can we deliver on our mission in new and different ways, ways that will attract new clients and make our existing clients even happier?" Daniel's process had served Jewel well.

Jewel is a wholesale distribution company, not a technology firm. Their technology—a major competitive advantage—gave them the ability to respond to individual client requests with an ease none of their competitors have yet to achieve.

At last year's Planning Day, the leadership team recognized how valuable their scheduling system was and suggested they start actively marketing it. The idea was Andy's, the heart and soul of Jewel's IT department. Andy's idea, creation, and design brought eight new clients last year, one of them a Fortune 500 company, and twenty million in new revenue, which helped them break $100 million in sales for the first time.

Once they were finished talking through last year's plan and some of the team's desires for the coming year, Daniel said, "I've got some news for everyone that is going to affect next year's road map."

An unexpected wrench in the Planning Day machine and Daniel had their attention. "Andy and I have been talking, and I think it's time to let you all know that he's planning to leave in a few months, at the end of our fiscal year."

The room went silent, faces paled, and Andy's absence became conspicuous. Daniel saw the impact of the news in posture and facial expression. The leadership team was not quite sure what to do or say. *Okay, I've got their attention. Now for the rest of the story.*

Mary Diamond, director of Human Resources, spoke first.

"Uh, Daniel, uh, I'm numb. I need to say something and don't know what to say. I-I-I'm… What happened?" she stumbled through. Mary was clearly troubled, as were most of the rest of the leadership team.

Chip, the man who never struggled for words, said, "Wh-wh-what, uh… That's, uh… I don't know what to say either. This is incredible. What happened? Why is he leaving? What are we going to do?"

Daniel responded, "Any one of us could be gone in an instant, including me. We were successful before Andy, we can be successful after. He's given us, all of us, an opportunity to see what we can do with technology. Now it's time for us to pick up our game and take it to the next level. Let's not squander what we've accomplished just because we're losing one person. We need to be resilient enough to survive these kinds of changes because they come along every day. The question is, what are we going to do about it?"

Daniel had achieved his goal. This year's Planning Day was not going to be just another Block of Cheese day.

"Folks, listen up, please." Daniel knew he had to be careful now that he'd put everyone in a state of disbelief and taken away their sense of stability. "Every year we go through this exercise and I know several of you don't like it. We do it for a very simple reason, and you all know why.

"We live in a world of change. That's why one of our core values is that 'we embrace change.' Whether we like it or not, change happens. Whether it's done unto us or we do it unto others, it's a reality we must embrace. We cannot afford to turn a blind eye and ignore the reality that everything in our world changes all the time.

"And every year when we go through this exercise, we evaluate our business, look for ways to fix problems, do better, be a better company. Lately, I've noticed that we've fallen into a nasty routine that can have devastating consequences. Anybody want to guess what I'm talking about?"

"It feels too easy," said one person.

"Easy, hell, it's too damn hard and getting harder. We need to find a way to ease some of the pressure!" said another.

"I didn't think we were having any financial issues, are we, Daniel?"

"Is there a problem with some of the departments meeting their budgets?"

"Is there a client problem we don't know about?"

"No, none of those things," Daniel said. "What we've got is a failure to recognize."

"Recognize? Recognize what?" was the general reaction.

This was his chance. *Make the point right and we win, screw it up and...*

"We fail to recognize all the things we take for granted. All the assumptions we make every day. All the places where change creates risk that we're not aware of or prepared for. Like having Andy resign."

He knew by the expressions in the room he had their attention.

"Andy's not leaving," he paused, "but one of these days, whether in seven months or seven years, we could suffer the loss of key people along with any number of other changes that could suddenly occur without warning. We need to be prepared. How many of the decisions we made in our road map last year were based on assumptions? How many of the issues we've discussed so far today are based on assumptions that everything will remain the same? Will we be prepared?"

Relief and understanding filled the room. The point had been made—staff were engaged and ready to go back to work on the business plan.

The organization depicted in this anecdote had struggled for years to institutionalize the business planning process with substantial resistance. Once they completed defining their purpose statements, vision, mission, and values, the planning process developed a different level of acceptance by staff.

The purpose statements gave them wide avenues to pursue new and different products and services, and the business plan became the one-year proving ground for new ideas and tweaking existing operations. The attitude toward participation shifted from avoidance to privilege among those who were invited to participate each year.

*****

Creating Your Business Plan

Planning is an unnatural process; it is much more fun to do something. The nicest thing about not planning is that failure comes as a complete surprise, rather than being preceded by a period of worry and depression.

—Sir John Harvey Jones[40]

Businesses consist of many interdependent people, functions, and activities. From operations including finance, fulfillment, and human resources to external support from vendors, financial institutions, and public services entities. Managing these entities can feel like a cage fight. Leadership and staff have an obligation to periodically review everything they do, identify opportunities for improvement,

---

[40] Jones, Sir John Harvey. "20142-John_Harvey_Jones," AZ QUOTES, https://www.azquotes.com/author/20142-John_Harvey_Jones.

and prepare for when, not if, something goes wrong. Something always goes wrong. If it doesn't, you're not trying hard enough.

A good business plan will always involve change.

The planning process is an ideal opportunity to survey staff and look for new things to try. A good starting point is to gather individuals from each operational area with depth of knowledge and experience along with a handful of creative newbies for outside-the-box ingenuity. Discuss what's worked well over the past year and what hasn't while looking for flawed assumptions. Talk about ways to collaborate, improve weaknesses, reinforce strengths, and become more efficient in the coming year.

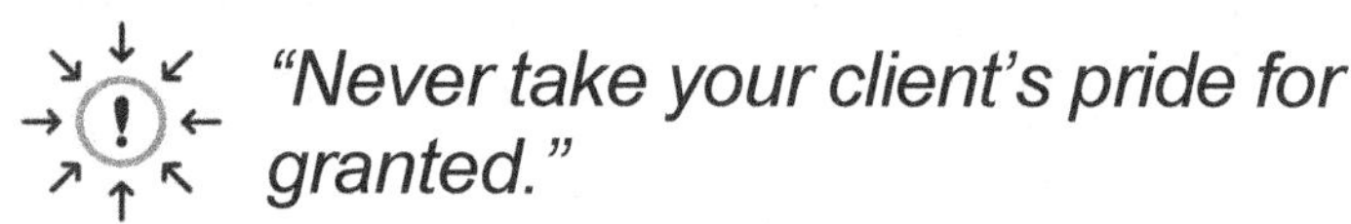

Explore opportunities to create competitive advantages with existing resources. What can your business do for your clients that your competitors can't or won't? What would be appreciated and seen as having valuable vendor insight? Never take your client's pride for granted. They want to work with successful companies known for dependability and forward-thinking. Positioning yourself that way creates loyalty that's hard for the competition to derail.

When finished, be sure to formalize your decisions in your business plan. Capture the goals and objectives along with the resources to pursue them and milestones to quantify their progress,

A strong and healthy business will always strive to prepare, improve, and expand, even if everything in your business appears to be status quo with no changes on the horizon. Change is coming. The business plan process will help management define how to proactively incorporate new knowledge, learn from experience, and adapt to a changing world.

A good business plan will clearly communicate the current year's business goals and objectives and how to achieve them.

A common understanding of the goals and objectives helps ensure everyone understands their importance. It explains how success will be measured and the role each employee will play in achieving them. This common understanding creates alignment and eliminates randomness, and wasted time and effort. When people can see how everything is connected, the results validate the idea of a team being greater than the sum of its parts.

On February 2, 2021, a Google search for "create business plan" found "about 199,000 results." How can there be 199,000 different resources to create something as common as a business plan? While there is more than one way to fry an egg, I doubt you can find 199,000.

If you've ever been casually talking and asked to "say that again," you know how difficult it can be to repeat yourself verbatim. While it can be easy to restate your point, using the exact same words is harder without having them in writing.

The physical act of writing your business plan triggers subconscious concerns about whether the eventual reader, whom you may never know or see, will understand your message the way you intend. We use greater care with the words we choose when we want people to understand. Thinking through and documenting what you want to convey results in clarity of thought, precise communication, and greater audience comprehension.

One of the inconvenient truths I've observed is that organizations who put their goals and desires in writing usually achieve them. Those leaders who keep plans in their heads usually don't. There are many reasons individuals and organizations have a hard time creating a business plan. Here are a few:

- We're busy; it's too time-consuming.
- They never seem to get implemented.
- Change is happening too fast.
- They don't have the clarity of purpose to create one.

Traditional components

Different audiences have different needs and wants. Diverse groups of stakeholders want the most relevant information about your company as it relates to their specific interests and concerns, and they want it presented in order of their priorities. One business plan cannot effectively serve all of them even though much of the raw data is identical. The three stakeholder groups every business eventually needs to write a plan for are the staff, banker, and investor.

The most important plan you will ever write is the internal plan for you and your staff. Their primary concern should be the current goals and objectives and how management wants to achieve them. To use a sports metaphor, they need to know what play is being called so they can execute properly.

Your banker's primary concern is your financial health. You need a plan for your banker because no business should ever be caught by uncontrollable circumstances that can disrupt cash flow. The best way to do that is to develop a strong relationship with a traditional bank.

> *"If you can't communicate the value of your business in terms an investor can connect with, odds are, you haven't a complete picture of what your business has to offer."*

The investor plan is where I usually get pushback because many businesses don't have traditional external investors whose primary interests are returns on their investments and realistic exit strategies. However, examining your business from an investor's perspective is an important element of good planning. If you can't communicate the value of your business in terms an investor can connect with, odds are, you haven't a complete picture of what your business has to offer.

For the investor, the first thing they'll want to see is the track record of your leadership team and whether they previously demonstrated the ability to succeed in similar roles. If that history is missing, the investor will likely tip his/her hat and say goodbye.

There are a handful of sections most business plans typically include[41]

- executive summary;
- overview of the business;
- history;
- mission, vision, and values;
- leadership team;
- organizational structure;
- products and services;
- current environment;
- SWOT[42] analysis;
- competitive analysis;
- customer profiles;
- technology;
- external environment;
- federal considerations and policy drivers;
- state considerations and policy drivers;
- goals and objectives;
- financials;
- three-year financial projections; and
- sales strategy.

Implementing Your Business Plan

Turning words on paper into action requires more than saying, "Read this and do it!" Staff must know and understand your business plan in the same clear, consistent manner with which it was

---

[41] Please see chapter 8—how does the business sell products and services: marketing plans for the reasons why a marketing plan is not listed here.

[42] SWOT: Strengths, Weaknesses, Opportunities, and Threats.

conceived regardless of who is presenting it. The business plan must be reviewed on a regular schedule and consulted when your organization faces operational decisions whose impacts are ambiguous or when the best course of action is unclear.

There are four guidelines for successful implementation and achievement of the objectives defined therein:

1. Every business plan involves change; *embrace* the change.
2. Recognize the business plan is more than a plan; it's a navigation and communications tool. *Use* the tool.
3. It's often called a road map because it will help you get from where you are to where you want to be; *follow* the map.
4. Different audiences have different needs and interests; *tailor different plans to each audience.*

Success requires understanding, practice, and mastery. The business plan must be referenced and discussed on a regular and consistent basis to ensure it is top-of-mind and used to help guide decisions and actions when ambiguity or questions arise.

Staff must believe leadership assigns value and importance to the business plan as a "guiding tool" and is committed to following it. They need to believe the company's business plan is an essential document to leadership and leadership is serious about following it.

Take your plan off your desk and encourage managers to discuss it with staff. Talking about it with them affords a variety of influential benefits.

1. Everyone gets to ask clarifying questions; management gets to ensure understanding.
2. Change is presented as part of a thoughtful, well-conceived plan supported by leadership with specific reasons and measures of success. (Knowing the benefits embedded in change is a powerful persuader.)
3. The whys and hows of changes being implemented can be explained.

4. Create awareness that changes will be monitored for targeted benefits.
5. Management can prepare staff for the difficulty of change and expressly convey their support while new skills are developed.
6. Reinforce the team aspect by conveying success depends on everyone's ability to execute the plan.

Too many businesses, both large and small, invest hundreds, sometimes thousands, of hours to create plans that are never seen or opened until the next annual planning meeting. A business plan not implemented will never achieve its objectives. An extraordinary plan is of little value if it gathers dust, as is too often the reality. How much impact can any plan have if it's never used? If a business decides to operate without a plan, it can easily become lost when the unexpected occurs or plans are disrupted, which, for most businesses, is more the norm than the exception.

Maintaining Your Business Plan

A good business plan retains relevance throughout its duration. Ensuring relevance requires three aspects of upkeep:

1. Institutionalizing a cyclical review and refresh effort
2. Adjusting when inaccurate core assumptions are identified
3. Adherence to the plan

Each business plan review and refresh cycle should include an examination of processes, procedures, and any assumptions they may be based on. Over time, it's easy for assumptions to grow in acceptance and be presumed to be facts. Identifying operational aspects of the business based on assumptions allows your organization to prepare for surprises when those "facts" end up being inaccurate or unrealized assumptions.

My clients occasionally ask how they're supposed to follow the business plan when the environment they're operating in is always changing. "Doesn't that mean we need to adjust what we're doing, rather than just following the business plan?" They're right, of course. It would be foolish to be guided by a document that involved living, moving parts without ever considering the need for adjustments.

The business plan was written by smart people making thoughtful decisions. It needs to be followed until core assumptions or realities change substantially or if efforts to achieve objectives clearly aren't working as expected. Don't forget the first leadership guideline: every business plan involves change; embrace the change.

A business plan is a powerful learning and organizational development tool. Embrace it with eagerness and tell stories about the wins it gives birth to over the years. When your business culture begins to embrace and depend on the planning and implementation processes of your business plan, you will be well on the way to a profitable, sustainable business.

Reflecting on the Business Plan

This chapter describes a new and different way to think about business plans for many leaders. To survive, businesses need to reinforce their abilities to thrive and grow. Whether your business needs to create, implement, or maintain a business plan, the following questions will help reveal their potential and identify clever ways to apply and capitalize on this vital tool:

- How do you know your business plan matches client needs and wants?
- What are a few creative ways you can improve involvement by actively using a business plan? What about planning? What about foresight or resource utilization or any of the other benefits mentioned in this chapter?
- Does your organization *have* a business plan?
- Is it documented, not in someone's head?
- Is it understood, embraced, and executed by leadership and staff?
- How do you know?

Accessing and completing the Index scorecard survey is explained in chapter 12.

Key Points

Ch 1	Operational Imperatives	Clarity of purpose	Consistency of performance	Engagement of people
Ch 2	Stage of Maturity	Youth	Adolescence	Adulthood
Ch 2	Why leaders fail to achieve the 3 Ps	They didn't know they needed to do them.	They didn't know how to do them.	They forgot they needed to do them.
Ch 3	Arc of Success	New Ideas ► Growth ► Complexity ►Controls ► Less Flexibility		
Ch 3	Problems with Success	Symptoms masquerading as root problems	Historically good operational behaviors that begin to create undesirable results	Emotional resistance to beneficial change
Ch 3	Index Indicators & (chapter #)	Values (4) Vision (5) Mission (6)	**Business Plan (7)** Marketing Plan Goals and Responsibilities	Systems and Structure Communications Plan

The business plan is one of the eight leading indicators of organizational success and sustainability. Leadership teams that care about long-term survival of their organizations should build and deploy all eight. Proper deployment requires strict adherence to the following four principles for each:

Index principle 1: Must exist in writing.
Index principle 2: Must be clearly and accurately
understood.
Index principle 3: Must be shared with the appropriate
people at the appropriate times.
Index principle 4: Must be embraced, modeled,
and used by leadership and staff.

Documenting your business goals and desires, while sometimes difficult and time-consuming, is *the* most effective action you can take to ensure they are achieved.

The rapid pace of change and diversity in the workplace presents a continuous stream of complex issues. The time and energy required to effectively recognize, plan for, and respond to these issues is beyond the capacity of what any business can be prepared to handle without a proper plan.

A good business plan will always involve change. Regular review and refresh of your plan is an opportunity to try new things too valuable to ignore and help ensure your organization can achieve them in a timely manner.

A good business plan will clearly communicate the current year's business goals and how to achieve them. It explains the objectives and their value, ensuring they can be understood. It explains how success will be measured and the role each employee will play in achieving it. This common understanding creates alignment and eliminates randomness, and wasted time and effort. When people can see how everything is connected, the results validate the idea of a team being greater than the sum of its parts.

Common business plan sections are as follows:

- Executive summary
- Overview of the business
- History

- Mission, vision, and values
- Leadership team
- Organizational structure
- Products and services
- Current environment
- SWOT analysis
- Competitive analysis
- Customer profiles
- Technology
- External environment
- Federal considerations and policy drivers
- State considerations and policy drivers
- Goals and objectives
- Financials
- Three-year financial projections
- Sales strategy

Note: Please see chapter 8 for why your marketing plan should be a stand-alone document, not embedded in your business plan.

Creating a good business plan is a skill that requires training and practice. Many people simply don't have the innate ability to do good planning. Teach the skill, practice the skill, and refine the skill so you and those who participate in the planning process can master it.

Seven primary benefits of a business plan are as follows:

- Foresight
- Engagement
- Alignment of staff
- Planning
- Communication
- Resources
- Financial

CHAPTER 8

Finding Customers: Marketing Plans

Index Indicator #5

A business without sales is not a business; it's a fulfillment department.

Business development encompasses three interdependent activities that potentially lead to revenue: public relations, marketing, and sales. Maintaining sales momentum requires continuously reminding your target markets of the benefits of doing business with you. That's the primary role of marketing—to create and reinforce top-of-mind awareness that drives individuals and organizations in need of your offerings to your business.

> **For Those with Marketing Chops?**
>
> This chapter covers marketing, one of the most basic and common facets of business. For those with marketing experience, consider moving on to some of the concepts you're less familiar with. When you've finished the book, come back and look for twists on common concepts and an idea or two that sparks something new for you.

Marketing fulfills a vital role in achieving consistency of performance, the second of the 3Ps. As such, it is also the fifth of eight Index indicators. I have found no connection between sustainability and public relations or sales. Many sustainable businesses abstain from public relations, and many failed businesses have a track record of sales strength.

A Bit of Taoism[43] [dou-iz-*uh*m]

I see a strong correlation between marketing plans and verse 11[44] of the Tao.

> Thirty spokes are joined together in a wheel,
>> but it is the center hole
>> that allows the wheel to function.
> We mold clay into a pot,
>> but it is the emptiness inside
>> that makes the vessel useful.
> We fashion wood for a house,
>> but it is the emptiness inside
>> that makes it livable.
> We work with the substantial,
>> but the emptiness is what we use.

Much like the wheel, the pot, and the house, the value of marketing plans is in the containers they create for developing and executing your marketing efforts.

Needs

Unlike the benefits of the other seven Index indicators, marketing plans are the only indicator dependent on external research. This external dependency introduces needs, rather than benefits. Needs that must be fulfilled for the indicator to be useful. The creation and maintenance of these indicators require four research activities:

---

[43] "The philosophical system evolved by Lao-tzu and Chuang-tzu, advocating a life of complete simplicity and naturalness and of noninterference with the course of natural events, in order to attain a happy existence in harmony with the Tao." Taoism. 2019. In dictionary.com. Retrieved September 8, 2019. https://www.dictionary.com/browse/taoism?s=t.

[44] "A Pot is Useful for its Emptiness," Retrieved August 25, 2019. http://tao-in-you.com/a-pot-is-useful-for-its-emptiness/.

market research, designation of target markets, measuring market demand, and understanding the competition.

Market research

Good marketing plans are built with thorough, quality market research. Logic can identify likelihoods, and probabilities can guide research efforts. Gathering data directly from customers and prospects within your target markets will always provide the best information.

Primary market research[45] is how your deliverables are refined and the seeds of sales are germinated. Without it, your business machine is at   risk of spinning its wheels or skidding off its intended path. Eliminating market research to save time or money often results in greater expense and wasted time than it takes to gather in the first place. Sometimes it can be destructive.

> ## What Is Business Development?
>
> For the purposes of this book, I use business development as a label for three activities.
>
> - Public relations— communicating the value your business offers to a broad audience that may or may not have a direct need, creating public awareness.
> - Marketing—communicating the value your business offers to people who may need it and may be willing to pay for it.
> - Sales—converting prospects into clients.

When done with concern and attention to detail, market research allows you to develop sound strategies and successful tactics that lead to efficient and sustainable sales activities. The first infor-

---

[45] "Primary research is research you conduct yourself (or hire someone to do for you). It involves going directly to a source—usually customers and prospective customers in your target market—to ask questions and gather information." Primary research. The Hartford Business Owner's Playbook. Retrieved September 28, 2019. https://www.thehartford.com/business-insurance/ strategy/market-research/primary-second-research.

mation your research needs to identify and verify is the demographics of your target markets.

Target markets

Few businesses are equipped to sell anything to everyone everywhere. Successful marketing requires identification of your ideal customer and understanding them. Narrowing the focus from everyone to those most likely to need your products and/or services allows for fine-tuning messaging, which results in reduced costs, increased wins in competitive situations, and better long-term customers.

The question to be answered is who are the organizations and individuals that want or need what your business offers. Once you've identified these most likely consumers of your offerings, you need to find out how much they need them and how badly they want them.

Market demand

Sales are fueled by need and driven by want, the yin and yang of market demand. Intellectuals focus on needs, while successful marketing wizards focus on wants (i.e., emotion). A common rookie mistake is assuming need alone motivates buyers. If that were true, cigarettes and obesity would not exist.

Caution is appropriate here; focusing on needs can appear as if the seller is taking advantage of the buyer who, theoretically, has no choice. Fulfilling wants is like giving people presents. I prefer catering to wants over needs because emotional wants can usually dominate physical needs. Want beats need except when time is short or pressure is great. *Even then, want often wins.*

While need can override emotion at times, the ideal approach is to position your offerings in terms of what your market wants while giving them what they need. Using a COVID-19 related example, assume you're an office furniture supply company. Finding prospects who need new furniture can be tough. By connecting that need to wanting remote workers back in the office and using new furniture as an incentive, the sale becomes easier and faster. When needs and wants are both served, demand is created.

As your business grows, so do your operating costs. Customer retention is the only way to leverage the high cost of each first sale to a new customer and the costs of growth to create economies of scale that offset them. Retention means every customer should be a repeat customer regardless of how often they buy. Retaining customers is easier with a robust knowledge of the competition.

Competition

Competitive information provides critical insight into demand and how the market values your offerings. Once you understand how the competition markets and prices their offerings, you gain insight into what the market wants and buys. It also aids in positioning your products and services so they stand apart. The goal is to make your competitors irrelevant by offering more compelling value and being top-of-mind.

Your competition is more than entities like yours selling the same products and services. It includes all companies serving the wants and needs your firm serves regardless of what they're selling. When searching for these outside-the-box alternatives, ask *where your clients would look for solutions* if your business wasn't there. Every one of those options competes for your client's dollars.

Another source of competition lives in the wants of your prospects. When a purchase is driven by want, other wants in the mind of your prospect will always compete for those same dollars. This makes marketing that focuses on wants without considering needs more vulnerable to competitive forces.

"*...marketing that focuses on wants without considering needs (is) more vulnerable to competitive forces.*"

At the end of the day, if what you're selling speaks to your prospects' wants, meets their needs, and is priced based on their perceived value, you've eliminated the stumbling blocks you can control. At that point, making the sale becomes a straightforward process and an exercise in connecting with buyers.

*****

Rick's Anecdote
The Entrepreneurs' Dream

You have to learn the rules of the game. Then you have to play better than everyone else.

—Albert Einstein[46]

As Rick came out from under the hybrid Mercedes SUV, he thought to himself, *This is the last Benz I'm gonna work on and make more money for someone else than myself. And where do they get off calling these things SUVs anyway?*

Rick Sanway was a mechanic. He knew as much about BMWs and Mercedes as the engineers who designed them; some would say more. Rick had been working on them for the same specialty German auto repair shop for fourteen years and was tired of getting paid a fraction of what the shop was charging for his time.

After watching all the mistakes the shop had made, Rick was confident he could do better. He'd been thinking about opening his own shop for years, and as he finished his current repair ticket, he realized that time was now.

Today was the day he was going to open his own shop and do things the right way. Rick had been saving his money and found a closed gas station in his neighborhood that would be perfect. Even

---

[46] Einstein, Albert. "Albert Einstein > Quotes > Quotable Quote," *Goodreads*. Goodreads Inc. https://www.goodreads.com/quotes/118785-you-have-to-learn-the-rules-of-the-game-and.

better, it was available for lease at a good price. He knew what to charge for his labor, and he knew all the auto-parts places he would need for parts and machine work. Sanway felt he had everything worked out and was ready to take the plunge.

He had flyers printed for his grand opening and specials to attract customers to his shop. Rick enlisted his niece, Molly, a computer whiz who talked a lot about Facebook, Spotify, Pinterest, YouTube, and a bunch of other web stuff he didn't really understand. She even set up a Facebook website and several ads for him that promoted his business.

Grand opening day came, and Rick felt like he was about to burst with joy over his new business, a dream come true. As the first hour passed and nobody came, he began to get nervous while doubt crept into his thoughts.

Where is everybody?

The second hour passed after what felt like twenty.

Are the address and phone number wrong on my material?

By lunchtime, Rick was calculating how long his savings would last if he didn't start getting some customers. He'd never thought about what would happen if he opened and nobody came.

That first day open was one of the most difficult days of Rick's life. It was also a sign of many similar days yet to come. By the end of the third week, he'd had two new customers who were both thrilled to find him. Unfortunately, at this pace, he wasn't going to be able to survive. He decided to call someone he'd met at a community college accounting class several years earlier, a woman named Jesse who had been in marketing and seemed to be very smart.

When Jesse came over to the shop, she was able to quickly uncover the gaps in Rick's plan. Once she realized Rick had the technical knowledge to do the work, she started probing his approach to marketing.

"How far did most of your customers at your last job travel to bring their vehicles to you?" she asked.

"I really don't know. We never talked about that," Rick responded.

"Five miles, ten miles, you know your customers, how far do you think they would travel to get to you if their car broke down?"

Rick had absolutely no clue. It was a thought that had never entered his conscious mind, and he told Jesse so.

"Jesse, I'm a bit embarrassed to say, I really honestly have no clue."

"Okay. Let's use me as an example. I don't want to have to travel out of my way for anything, and when my car has a problem, I'm already unhappy, which makes it even worse to have to go out of my way to get it looked at, much less fixed.

"The first thing I look for is a shop that's close to a route I take often, like to the grocery store. If I can't find anything, I'll start looking in the general direction of where I usually travel. Most of my trips are less than ten miles, so let's see how many BMWs and Mercedes are registered within a ten-mile radius of your shop."

Jesse knew that data was readily available from several sources for a small fee. Rick agreed, and Jesse went after the info. She found a total of two BMWs and zero Mercedes registered with an address within ten miles of Rick's new shop.

He had made a classic entrepreneurial mistake. He forgot to identify the size of his market. Rick could have opened the best repair shop this side of the Mississippi and he still wouldn't get enough business to keep the doors open.

This sad story repeats itself all too often when companies, even mature and successful ones, open or launch new products and services. There's more data available today than ever before, data that helps ensure investments of time, money, and effort produce sufficient ROI. Introducing new items without accounting for the most relevant pieces of data is like trying to paint a garden full of beautiful blooming flowers using two colors—it's lifeless.

Creating Your Marketing Plan

A marketing plan describes something being offered for sale, prospective buyers, and instructions on how to put the two together in the hope of making a sale.

There are many ways to create a marketing plan and, like business plans, extensive resources for guidance. My addition to the massive volume of marketing plan development material begins with the premise that what you are selling—whether product, service, or combination—is a solution. Solutions either solve a specific problem or create a specific desired result.

Assume your solution addresses an inability to penetrate a particular market. You can describe the issue as a problem to be solved. "We struggle to sell in the southeastern states." You can also describe the same issue as a desired result to be realized. "We want to increase our sales in the southeastern states." This is one of the precarious nuances of messaging.

If the client is driven by fear, focus on solutions to problems. If the client is driven by wants, focus on desired results. Choosing whether to use problem versus result messaging produces unpredictable outcomes. According to Salesforce Training, "People are willing to run greater risks to avoid losses than they are to make gains."[47]

While this may lead you to conclude that fear is the best approach, both work well when properly executed. There is no simple or straightforward way to make that determination. The best approach for your needs depends on the contextual nuances of your organization and target markets.

Once you've identified the solutions you sell, present them with a three-part framework:

- Issue
- Evidence
- Impact

Document the issue(s) by describing the problem your solution eliminates or the desired result it creates. For each solution, provide evidence that objectively proves your claims even though many purchases are not made rationally. The last piece is to describe the impact

---

[47] Jeffrey, Brian. "Fear Sells, so Sell Fear." *Salesforce Training*, Salesforce Training, January 31, 2012. https://www.salesforcetraining.com/fear-sells-so-sell-fear/.

of the solution on your prospect's business. This is where you can leverage the emotional strings of wants to help close the sale.

Issues, evidence, and impact give you the who, what, why, and value of your solutions. What's left is to use your market research to set pricing,[48] build financial projections, and craft paths around and through the competition to communicate with the right prospects. When finished, you'll have a marketing plan that can hone your organization into a sales machine.

Two key details

Detail 1: Most businesses offer more than one product and serve more than one market. Different markets, products, and services require different strategies, tactics, and approaches for successful selling. Therefore, I strongly encourage you to have a marketing plan for each group of products and services that do not share the same customer demographics or cyclical characteristics.

Detail 2: Your marketing plans should be stand-alone documents, not embedded in your business plan. Different products, services, markets, and geographic regions have different cycles. Tax preparers focus on IRS deadlines; weather-related providers focus on the season. Because each marketing recipe has its own proprietary cycle, it doesn't make sense to embed them into the financially driven cycle of your business plan.

---

[48] One of the often overlooked and misunderstood characteristics of pricing is the amount of revenue each sale contributes to profit—also referred to as contribution margin. Contribution margin is calculated by deducting variable costs from revenue. While understanding and managing the contribution margin of your offerings can have a major impact on profitability and demand, consistently and accurately identifying variable costs needed to do so is more than complicated; it is complex.

Implementing Your Marketing Plan

A marketing plan is a fancy label for a project. Once the plan is complete, implementation begins the same way a project would be launched.

One individual should be assigned accountability for ensuring the plan is executed and activities must be assigned to specific staff. All activities need to be reviewed for dependencies and prioritized. Where multiple staff are working on the same activity, a single point of contact should be assigned to avoid confusion and ensure proper communication. This also helps everyone in your organization to know exactly who to contact when information is needed.

Each activity should also have several details associated with it:

- Specific, measurable objectives
- Start and completion dates
- Milestones

To ensure your marketing efforts are creating the desired results, a traditional project management tool should be used to monitor, measure, and manage activities throughout the course of the plan's execution. Doing so will provide the information needed to adjust any aspects that aren't creating the desired results.

Maintaining Your Marketing Plan

Marketing plans need to be maintained based on cycles of demand. These cycles are rarely connected to the ebbs and flows of business operations. Just because your business plan may cover a one-year period, your marketing plan duration may need to be longer or shorter, depending on demand cycles.

The most important aspect of marketing plan maintenance is the integration of continuous market research *while each plan is being executed.*

Having access to customers and prospects while marketing activities are conducted provides insight into their wants and needs in a way nothing else can match. Everyone involved with executing a marketing plan should be trained and prepared to look and listen for changes in the market your business will eventually need to react to. Having that advance notice gives you time to prepare and adjust your plans in advance of coming change. It's also where many competitive advantages are created.

Reflecting on Marketing Plans

This chapter describes a new and different way to think about marketing plans for most leaders. To survive, businesses need to reinforce their abilities to thrive and grow. Whether your business needs to create, implement, or maintain marketing plans, the following questions will help reveal their potential and identify clever ways to apply and capitalize on this vital tool:

- What are the products and services competing for your prospect's dollars? Not just the other competitive products/services, anything that may redirect their money away from your offerings.
- How well are your marketing efforts in sync with cyclical demands?
- What are a few creative ways you can better target your markets by actively using marketing plans? What about quantifying demand? What about market research or understanding your competition or any of the other benefits mentioned in this chapter?
- Does your organization *have* marketing plans?
- Are they documented, not in someone's head?
- Are they understood, embraced, and supported by leadership and staff and followed?
- How do you know?

Accessing and completing the Index scorecard survey is explained in chapter 12.

Key Points

Ch 1	Operational Imperatives	Clarity of purpose	Consistency of performance	Engagement of people
Ch 2	Stage of Maturity	Youth	Adolescence	Adulthood
Ch 2	Why leaders fail to achieve the 3 Ps	They didn't know they needed to do them.	They didn't know how to do them.	They forgot they needed to do them.
Ch 3	Arc of Success	New Ideas ► Growth ► Complexity ► Controls ► Less Flexibility		
Ch 3	Problems with Success	Symptoms masquerading as root problems	Historically good operational behaviors that begin to create undesirable results	Emotional resistance to beneficial change
Ch 3	Index Indicators & (chapter #)	Values (4) Vision (5) Mission (6)	Business Plan (7) **Marketing Plans (8)** Goals and Responsibilities	Systems and Structure Communications Plan

Solutions either solve a specific problem or create a specific desired result.

The three ingredients for creating a compelling solution are

- issue,
- evidence, and
- impact.

Marketing plans almost always cover a period of time different and disconnected from the typical operational cycles of a business;

therefore, they should be stand-alone documents, not incorporated into business plans.

Most businesses have multiple offerings serving multiple markets with varying needs and interests. The need to accommodate these variations to ensure success typically requires multiple marketing plans.

Four sets of research data that make marketing plans effective are as follows:

- Market research
- Target markets
- Market demand
- Competition

CHAPTER 9

Who Empties the Trash:
Goals and Responsibilities
Index Indicator #6

A common reality among managers is, day-to-day operations demand more time than there is to give. Asking them to commit additional time and energy to tracking and monitoring the details that make their businesses work is tantamount to bleeding the dead. Initially, routine can be comforting. Over time, and without thought, familiarity breeds complacency that inevitably leads to costly bad habits and crippling assumptions.

In one of Gallagher's comedy routines, he describes answering his front doorbell and handing a package to the man standing at the door. When he returned to the living room, his nine-year-old daughter asked, "Who was that?"

Gallagher replied, "The UPS man."

"How can you be *sure*?" she asked.

At each stage of organizational development, your successful company will experience certain predictable changes as it cycles through the Arc of Success.[49] While it may seem counterintuitive, without change, you have no growth. But if change is constant, all you have is instability, and that's no way to thrive. Therein lies the

---

[49] From the "Arc of Success" in chapter 2: Experience provides the bricks that pave the road to maturity. Each stage of maturity, youth, adolescence, and adulthood is achieved as organizations journey through predictable changes described by the Arc of Success: new ideas, growth, complexity, controls, lost flexibility.

rub. There is great value in creating routines and ensuring they're being followed. Goals and responsibilities (G&R) are the third and final fundamental component of the second "P," performance.

Benefits

Creating, documenting, and implementing goals and responsibilities has five primary benefits: accountability, balancing responsibility and authority, appropriate workloads, contribution to marketing, and retention.

Accountability

It can be difficult to operate without clearly defined and documented G&R. Ensuring tasks are done properly and timely requires someone to be accountable for every operational need. Routine activities aren't usually difficult to cover. Infrequent activities can be neglected and become destructive when a valued client's trust is undermined or failure to fulfill legal obligations becomes expensive.

An ad hoc approach to getting things done simply doesn't scale. When a business is small, everybody knows one another and what needs to be done. Needs are fulfilled by anyone who has the time for them. As the organization grows, changes and troubling issues tend to arise.

Familiarity among staff diminishes, and what others do become less clear. The risk of important tasks falling through the cracks grows while the potential for duplication of effort increases. The ability to manage and measure performance becomes more complex and difficult to master. The mere potential for these problems to arise often leads to an erosion of morale.

Creating a positive environment where accountability is valued and embraced requires proper balancing of authority and responsibility.

Balancing responsibility and authority

Imagine a teeter-totter. On one end, an eight-year-old girl; on the other, her father. While the dad and the daughter both want the same result, that teeter-totter isn't moving unless the dad pushes up. Balanced? Not quite.

When you assign responsibility without commensurate authority, your assignee is destined to face insurmountable barriers. The problem is magnified when coworkers with similar constraints are asked to help as assignees recognize their inability to execute the task. Any such imbalance turns responsibility from a potential morale booster into a morale buster.

Having clear goals and responsibilities helps eliminate built-in failure by allowing for responsibilities and authority that are clear, balanced, and transparent to the entire organization. Balance is not enough. You must also provide proper training and sufficient time.

Appropriate workloads

No two people have the same knowledge or abilities. Ensuring workloads are properly distributed helps minimize burnout, produce consistent performance, and create expected outcomes so clients have predictable, dependable experiences.

Having specific measurable G&R assigned to specific individuals in specific departments, supervisors and managers can ensure each individual is responsible for an equitable and achievable workload. It also allows for burden sharing of the least pleasant tasks.

Before technology was so prevalent, I've known public relations firms to gather all staff to help assemble mailings for clients, a thankless task few enjoy, sharing the burden among everyone, even the boss, *and* saving money. This type of group effort relieves the pressure of their daily grind and gives everyone opportunities to work together, creating wins they can proudly share.

Contribution to marketing

Clearly describing every staff member's opportunities to market and sell, whether proactively or passively, helps them understand and recognize the importance of a coordinated, unified marketing and sales culture. Explicitly giving individuals a range of these opportunities beyond their daily routines helps connect them to the organization's success and feel better about their part in it.

Creating a role for everyone in the success of the business makes their job more enjoyable and creates a better working environment. It also helps leverage investments in staff by improving their ability to contribute. When people feel they're contributing to its success, it creates an emotional desire to continue, which leads to retention of staff.

Retention

Describing G&R helps employees understand what is valued and expected of them. The simple act of documenting expectations has the remarkable effect of increasing the likelihood of achievement. When expectations are achieved and noticed, opportunities are created for management to recognize staff and reward them.

From the smallest mom-and-pop shop to the largest high-tech corporations, employees come and go because of the way they're treated. Research has proven most people leave their jobs because of a bad manager or hostile work environment, not compensation. Simply put, employees come and go because of the way they're treated.

Clarity of individual G&R allows for discussion when issues, problems, or conflicts arise. It becomes easier to communicate and find positive resolutions through common ground. Common ground is how mutual respect and relationships are developed, partnerships are built, and collaboration becomes joyful. Enjoyment creates an emotional draw that attracts people.

By defining the work individuals are being paid to do, you're proactively creating opportunities for them to grow and learn. You also begin to lay the foundation for developing the next level of organizational maturity.

Note: There's growing debate over the efficacy of a top-down management style vs. the enlightened alternative of self-management. I've found the active use of G&R to be critical for both.

As with all things worth doing, there are difficult and rewarding aspects to effectively creating and using them.

*****

Keith's Anecdote
The Case of the Duplicated Report

True terror is to wake up one morning and discover that your high school class is running the country.

—Kurt Vonnegut[50]

The leadership team included the general manager, three vice presidents, and four senior managers. When they needed some data, everyone knew it was in a familiar report they didn't have in the meeting. One of the vice presidents and one of the senior managers both stood and said, almost in unison, "I've got last month's report on my desk. I'll go get it."

Neither had distributed their report to the other. Both were surprised their colleague had a copy. Both left to fetch their copy. Both returned quickly with two different versions of the same data.

Everyone was familiar with one report or the other; no one had seen both.

Keith, one of the senior managers, asked Karlee, one of the vice presidents, where she got the report.

"I had my staff create it. They create it for me every month. We've been producing it since before I came on board. That's at least five years now."

---

50 Vonnegut Jr., Kurt. "Kurt Vonnegut Jr. > Quotes > Quotable Quote," *Goodreads*. https://www.goodreads.com/quotes/21895-true-terror-is-to-wake-up-one-morning-and-discover.

"Really, have you tracked how long it takes to produce?"

"Forty hours, give or take," she replied without hesitation.

Silence.

After a nervous silence while everyone regained their equilibrium, Keith spoke.

"Reeeeally" was all he could say.

After a few moments of absorption and reflection, Garry, the general manager, spoke.

"I assume no one has seen both reports, no one knew two people were creating the same report, correct?"

Every head in the room nodded.

"Keith, am I safe in assuming your team invests about forty hours each month creating your version?"

Keith nodded.

"Does everyone get a copy of one of these reports every month?" asked Garry.

Every head in the room nodded.

"Great, no one was aware two similar reports existed. Let's pass them around. Look for anything in one and not the other."

Several minutes later, Garry asked, "Did anyone see anything in one that wasn't in the other?"

Everyone shook their head.

"Is there any reason we're creating two reports and spending eighty or more hours when we could be spending forty?"

Again, every head in the room shook no.

"At forty hours for each report and two reports each month, one quarter of someone's annual salary is going straight down the drain. We have a problem, people. It's not major, and it is a slow bleed of time, one of our most precious, unrecoverable assets. How are we going to fix this?"

Keith said, "No one has enough time, and fixing this is simple. Karlee and I will figure out who's best positioned to produce the report and stop duplicating efforts. The bigger problem for me is, where else are we wasting time?"

"How do we gather and evaluate that information without wasting more time on minor, unimportant administrivia? If we're going to go through this process, we want to make sure it creates some return on our investment. At least that way, we can all make the best use of our time."

Creating Your Goals and Responsibilities

Creating G&R for everyone (yes, everyone) from the most senior executives (and board chair if the position exists) to the secretary can sound like a herculean task. Just talking about it can create high anxiety and unrest.

That's the bad news.

The good news: when you plan and execute well, results can be staggeringly positive and beneficial. Proper planning and cautious execution are critical to success, minimizing burden, and maximizing results.

The more common chain-of-command top-down model can be quite effective when used properly. Creation requires identification of primary points of contact throughout your organization and clear understanding of individual G&R. One of its greatest benefits is the ability to enculturate a manage-up mindset. Doing so enables

---

A Manage-Up Mindset

Organizational success is a prerequisite for sustainability, which is usually achieved by a dedicated team working together focused on a shared goal. Sustainability is greatly furthered when everyone is also striving to improve themselves. Unfortunately, managing up has attracted several negative connotations ranging from being manipulative or self-serving to support for weak, overworked, or incompetent managers.

While most business tactics can be harmful or dangerous in the wrong hands, I see managing up as a powerful and positive tool when executed properly. Harvard Business Review, among others, has published a post that highlighted the better side of managing up and referenced another perspective from Harvard Business Review.

Managing up is about using the traits of a good manager to help bring out the best in you as an employee. When done effectively, managing up makes your manager's job easier, as well as your day-to-day job.

The Harvard Business Review defines managing up as "being the most effective employee you can be, creating value for your boss and your company."[51]

---

[51] Croswell, Alexis. "Managing Up: What It Means and Why It's Important," Culture Amp. Pty. Ltd., https://www.cultureamp.com/blog/managing-up-importance.

staff to shatter the barriers inherent in a traditional chain of command environment.

Successful efforts launch as a formal change management initiative with project planning, sponsors, and written communication plans. These proven techniques should be mandatory, not optional.

The creation process begins with the identification of sponsors, the best active and visible authority figures from each department or operational area. The goal of each sponsor is to demonstrate management's support for, and commitment to, the effort. Similar to a project manager, each sponsor's goals include ensuring availability of training, guidance, and support needed to properly document everyone's G&R.

Sponsors direct staff within their span of control to document what they do each day for one month. When assigning the task, the added workload must be balanced with existing duties and obligations while due dates are adjusted to minimize disruption.

> *"Instruct staff to focus on what they're expected to achieve (goals), not what they're expected to do (tasks)."*

Instruct staff to focus on what they're expected to achieve (goals), not what they're expected to do (tasks). To illustrate the difference, a task might be "Empty the trash." When defined as a goal, it might be "Keep the office clean."

When going through this process, a helpful question for everyone to ask themselves is, "What do colleagues and customers depend on me for?" Don't let staff get caught in minutia or capturing too much detail. Remind them, they're not creating an instruction manual. Data such as frequency, duration, and instructions will be important when developing your systems and structure in chapter 10.

Once staff have identified their goals, sponsors must ensure managers review each list one-on-one with their staff. This process has five objectives:

1. Verify alignment with management's desires.[52]
2. Confirm documentation is clearly understood.
3. Identify performance measures.
4. Expose duplication of effort.
5. Schedule regular goals review and validation.

Note: Documenting and implementing G&R increases the value and benefits of having documented systems and structure (chapter 10).

Implementing Your Goals and Responsibilities

The measure of successful implementation of G&R is increased organizational sustainability throughout times of change regardless of how turbulent the environment becomes. Achieving that ability to handle change is dependent on two distinct aspects of implementation: First, direct reports, peers, and those you report to must all work together collaboratively. Second, everyone must share a common understanding that includes a commitment to common goals. An understanding leading to the realization that most, if not all, of everyone's coworkers are dependent in some way and, to some degree, on each other's success. I call this interdependence.

A "best practices" implementation begins with everyone reviewing their G&R with colleagues who depend on their achievement. One creative example of this comes from the Morningstar Company in Woodland, California, with approximately 350 full-time employees.

---

[52] This can be an ideal opportunity for staff to share new ideas and management to learn from the experience and knowledge of those most connected to the work being done. It can also be an opportunity to manage up.

Every year, each Morning Star employee negotiates a colleague letter of understanding (CLOU) with the associates who are most affected by his or her work. A CLOU (pronounced "clue") is, in essence, an operating plan for fulfilling one's mission. An employee may talk to ten or more colleagues during the negotiations, with each discussion lasting twenty to sixty minutes. A CLOU can cover as many as thirty activity areas and spells out all the relevant performance metrics. All together, CLOUs delineate roughly three thousand formal relationships among Morning Star's full-time employees.[53]

Whether you choose to follow Morningstar's model or a more traditional approach, I've identified four steps that make implementation easier:

1. Organize actions and activities supporting G&R into chronological order.
2. Group actions in a way that minimizes consumption of one or more of the three finite resources: people, time, and money.[54]
3. Assign each action to at least one staff member.
4. Identify one primary point of contact for each group of actions to ensure everyone in your organization knows exactly who to contact when information or updates are needed.[55]

Implementing G&R often involves numerous changes to who is responsible for what. One of the ancillary effects is the need to delegate, which can quickly become a major component of daily activity.

---

[53] Hamel, Gary. "First, Let's Fire All the Managers." *Harvard Business Review*, December 2011. 50–60 (provided by Noa Goihberg, HBR phone rep., 800.988.0886, 2/18/20 @ 10:35 a.m.).

[54] Grouping criteria is dependent on the products, services, organizational structure, and numerous other factors ranging from logistics to security.

[55] Identifying primary points of contact will be critical in the section on the 3rd "p," people, in both chapters 10 and 11, systems and structure and communication plans. Capturing this information during the development and implementation of G&R tends to be the easiest approach.

Delegation embodies aspects of power (sometimes in a subtle, surreptitious, or furtive manner) and should be approached with caution. The biggest risk with delegation is when responsibility is assigned without imbuing the delegate with enough authority to succeed.

For example, if you're assigned responsibility for data backup and security, you must have access to all the data within your organization, particularly the most sensitive (e.g., finances and personnel data). Without access, you'll be unable to validate the integrity of your backups or restore data when needed.

Accepting responsibility without adequate authority is the terrible real-world scenario where you find yourself between a rock and a hard spot. Begin with the assumption your level of authority is insufficient for your new responsibilities. Look for ways, with your superiors, to bring your authority into proper balance before you find yourself in a no-win situation.

There are several actions you can use to avoid becoming the problem for something you can't fix:

- When you are offered greater responsibility, first ask yourself why. What is it you will be expected to do, and was that expected before, or was it newly assigned to you along with the responsibility?
- Who was responsible before you, and why has the responsibility been shifted to you? Did someone lack the skills, resources, or perhaps the authority to be successful?
- Ask yourself what it will take for you to be successful in fulfilling your new responsibilities. Look for potential conflicts between sales and production, marketing and finance, front-line workers and management, and everyone and human resources.
- Identify those areas where you may not have enough authority to accomplish your new tasks. Look for alternatives to circumvent them.
- If you find yourself faced with this problem, talk to the individual who assigned your new responsibilities. Let him or her know how and where you're having problems and

work with them to identify solutions or negotiate additional authority.

If you accept new responsibility, you are probably doing a good job. Congratulations! Embrace the opportunity for personal growth, aka change, and focus on being successful.

Maintaining Your Goals and Responsibilities

Maintaining G&R becomes the necessary process of ensuring they create maximum value as inevitable change occurs in and around an organization. There are two times an active maintenance effort should be performed: First, during a regularly scheduled review and revise process. Repeat a few steps from the creating section with each list of roles and responsibilities or CLOU. Second, when a repetitive process or procedure is implemented, modified, or eliminated. For these situations, staff within two degrees of separation from the activity should be involved in the review and incorporation of the changes into their roles and responsibilities.

Reflecting on Goals and Responsibilities

This chapter describes a new and different way to think about individual goals and responsibilities for most leaders. To survive, businesses need to reinforce their abilities to thrive and grow. Whether your business needs to create, implement, or maintain goals and responsibilities, the following questions will help reveal their potential and identify clever ways to apply and capitalize on this vital tool:

- How do your managers avoid inappropriate extremes of micromanaging and insufficient guidance and support?
- How do you know when demands on individuals have exceeded their capacity?
- What are a few creative ways you can maintain and secure appropriate workloads by actively using goals and responsibilities? What about accountability? What about balancing

responsibility and authority or any of the other benefits mentioned in this chapter?

- Does your organization *have* goals and responsibilities?
- Are they documented, not in someone's head?
- Are they understood, embraced, and pursued by everyone?
- How do you know?

Accessing and completing the Index scorecard survey is explained in chapter 12.

Key Points

Ch 1	Operational Imperatives	Clarity of purpose	Consistency of performance	Engagement of people
Ch 2	Stage of Maturity	Youth	Adolescence	Adulthood
Ch 2	Why leaders fail to achieve the 3 Ps	They didn't know they needed to do them.	They didn't know how to do them.	They forgot they needed to do them.
Ch 3	Arc of Success	New Ideas ► Growth ► Complexity ►Controls ► Less Flexibility		
Ch 3	Problems with Success	Symptoms masquerading as root problems	Historically good operational behaviors that begin to create undesirable results	Emotional resistance to beneficial change
Ch 3	Index Indicators & (chapter #)	Values (4) Vision (5) Mission (6)	Business Plan (7) Marketing Plans (8) **Goals and Responsibilities (9)**	Systems and Structure Communications Plan

Without change, you have no growth. Without routine, you have no change. If change is constant, all you have is instability, and that's no way to thrive. There is great value in creating routines and ensuring they're being followed.

When properly practiced, managing up makes both the manager and direct report better.

The process of documenting systems and structure can be an ideal opportunity for staff to share new ideas and management to learn from the experience and knowledge of those most connected to the work being done. It can also be an opportunity to develop managing-up skills and practice them.

Five needs are fulfilled by documenting and implementing G&R:

1. Creating a positive environment where accountability is valued and embraced (accountability)
2. Eliminating built-in failure with a transparent authority commensurate with assigned responsibilities (balancing responsibility and authority)
3. Consistently meeting expectations and delivering predictable client experiences (appropriate workloads)
4. Telling staff where their opportunities to market and sell exist and how to use them (marketing)
5. Documenting expectations improves achievement of them along with creating opportunities for recognition and reward (retention)

Five primary benefits of goals and responsibilities are as follows:

- Accountability
- Balancing responsibility and authority
- Appropriate workloads
- Contribution to marketing
- Retention

PART 4

ADULTHOOD AND THE THIRD P: ENGAGEMENT OF PEOPLE

If your organization has made it through the first two stages of maturity, you and your team have survived the growth and changes that are the foundation of a successful, mature company. Congratulations. You have one more operational imperative to achieve to create sustainability.

Once adulthood is reached, survival depends on continuing to follow the guiding light of purpose, delivering consistent performance, and finding new ways to grow, each an endless pursuit. By the time most organizations have completed their first cycle of the Arc in adulthood, they've fully leveraged core strengths and value propositions to maximize growth. At that point, the greatest opportunities for growth tend to exist outside, and not too distant from, those core strengths.

One winning approach is expanding the depth or breadth of an existing value chain. The approach and/or efficacy of doing so depends on details outside the scope of this book. What's important is, this stage represents the time new, youthful efforts must be launched and begin cultivating their maturation in search of growth.

Recall one aspect of adolescence focuses on the individual and their responsibilities. In adulthood, focus shifts to the relationships of tasks and people to one another.[56] This shift is best handled by embracing proactive operational adjustments to structure, process, and the disruption that often accompany them.

Legislative mandates also become a greater burden in adulthood as the number of employees grows, which increases risk and liability. These realities are why the most mature organizations must rely heavily on engagement for sustainability.

The concept of engagement was skillfully discussed in a Harvard Business Review column by Ryan Fuller and Nina Shikaloff titled "Being Engaged at Work Is Not the Same as Being Productive," published February 16, 2017. In it, they state, "The holy grail of today's workplace is high employee engagement." It has simultaneously become the shibboleth of HR departments throughout the land.

While I agree engagement is critical, the problem with engagement being the desired objective for employees is clearly expressed in Fuller and Shikaloff's "word of caution": "*Engagement* is often an ambiguous term."

The two fundamental indicators of the third P, engagement of people, are systems and structure (S&S) and communication plans. First, clarity of systems and structure.

An understanding of how and where an employee's raw work product comes from and how and where it goes when they're done gives them a sense of their place in the big picture of company value. It creates connection, ownership, a sense of purpose, and control, all of which are part of what engagement attempts to encompass.

---

[56] See the "Goals and Responsibilities" and "Systems and Structure" comparison table in chapter 10.

Second, robust, clear, logically documented and accessible communication plans create an environment where communication flows smoothly and without friction. This allows for grievances to be communicated without fear of retaliation[57] and information to be disseminated to the appropriate people at the appropriate time, both of which are critical components of engagement that simultaneously empower.

---

[57] When staff is directed to communicate in a specific way and they do so, the employee has the protection of management's clear and explicit guidance. This is covered more thoroughly in chapter 11—Information Sharing: Communications Plan.

CHAPTER 10

How Work Flows through the Business: Systems and Structure

Index Indicator #7

This is the entry point to adulthood, where leadership becomes structurally disconnected from the customer for the first time. This is the point where growth cannot be sustained without the next layer of formality, systems and structure (S&S).

As businesses grow, the distance[58] between customer, staff, and operations that create products and deliver services also grows. The intimacy of relationships between leadership and customer is harder to maintain. Ensuring all the moving parts and pieces continue to create desired results becomes more difficult and complicated.

If there is going to be a failure point for an adolescent organization, G&R is where it typically starts because they cannot mature into adulthood without G&R. S&S is the most likely failure point for mature organizations.

---

[58] "The distance between customer, staff, and operations" refers to the organizational layers that separate leadership from their consumers. This distance exists because the responsibilities of leadership become consumed by strategic and operational demands and there is a finite number of hours in any day. In short, the role of leadership changes, and their priorities must shift from consumers to their organizations.

While G&R (outlined in chapter 9) and S&S are inherently connected, they are not codependent. The table below highlights some of the areas where G&R and S&S intersect and their differences.

Goals and Responsibilities (G&R)	Systems and Structure (S&S)
Focused on individuals and groups	Focused on connections and relationships
Unintentional duplications of effort; inefficiencies are hidden	Duplication by design; inefficiencies are exposed
Clear accountability	Same
Identify holes and gaps and eliminate them	Same
Document levels of authority and responsibility	Identify necessary levels of authority and responsibility
Balance workloads; create consistent, predictable capacities and outcomes	Same
Clarify expectations and dependencies create common ground and lead to staff development and succession preparedness	Same
Identifies primary points of contact	Locate ideal primary points of contact
Identify who needs what to trigger their work; driven by sponsors	Identify triggers that move work through the organization or slows it down
What is expected and by whom	Driven by primary points of contact
How work product moves through the organization	Same

Documenting S&S enables the creation of a bird's-eye view map of how data and work products are created, evolve, and flow through the organization. Such a map, occasionally referred to as a data flow diagram (DFD) or entity relationship diagram (ERD), becomes a powerful tool for creating engagement.

The burden of capturing all your S&S is far outweighed by the benefits.

Benefits

When people are financially invested, they want a return. When people are emotionally invested, they want to contribute.

—Simon Sinek[59]

Creating, documenting, and implementing systems and structure has four primary benefits: connection to purpose, connection to customers, teamwork and collaboration, and best practices.

Connection to purpose

As more people begin doing the same things to increase capacity, individuals can feel a diminishing sense of importance as they become hidden in the machine. Efforts to deliver on a macro scale can be demeaning to individuals and suppress the sense of value.

When individuals can see and understand how they contribute, how their efforts contribute to their organization's success, they can see and feel a sense of value and the frustration of apparent busy work goes away.

Mapping individual activities to sales, profits, and customer satisfaction definitively connects seemingly unrelated efforts directly to company goals. It explicitly shows how individual efforts help the organization deliver on its mission and pursue its vision while guided

---

[59] Sinek, Simon, "Quotes › Authors › S › Simon Sinek › When people are financially invested, they…" AZ QUOTES, https://www.azquotes.com/quote/700566.

by its values. It creates a sense of participation in the success of something bigger than themselves.

Connection to the customer

Serving the customer is the primary goal of every organization. What other reason is there for it to exist? The motivation is eternal—providing value results in some form of revenue that allows the organization to continue. Every organizational activity should contribute to that value. If it doesn't, it's a waste of time and money.

No organization can survive without customers. Public entities are paid for their services from tax revenues; not-for-profits are paid by donations and sales of products or services that contribute to each entity's specific purpose. There's no better way to demonstrate how organizations create and deliver value to their customers than by documenting your S&S and creating a graphic diagram for a big-picture view.

Teamwork and collaboration

Most people begin to see the big picture when they understand the full scope of output they're a part of. It begins with knowing how the documents and products they work on are created and delivered to them, then whom their work products are delivered to and what happens next. The result is the connection of individual actions and delivery of products and services to the ultimate customer.

The ability of every employee to do their job is dependent on someone else in the organization doing theirs, much like the way sports teams are dependent on each player fulfilling their designated role for team success. As a simple example, each member of a track relay team must hand the baton off to the next runner or the race for that team is over. If any member of the team fails to cleanly hand off the baton, the team has lost before the race finishes.

By understanding how each individual and activity within the organization contributes to delivery of value to the end user, there is an immediate recognition of how each person is dependent on others before and after him/her. This awareness creates an unambiguous sense of teamwork and recognition of the need for collaboration.

Best practices

An S&S diagram of your organization showcases how any single action impacts other actions. It helps find and solve problems faster and more effectively by showing the sequential path of any activity that produces a less-than-ideal result. It allows for refinement of who does what, in what sequence, and provides a traceable image of time wasters by showing when, where, and how data is handled more than once or delivered to people who don't need it.

> **"The ability of every employee to do their job is dependent on someone else in the organization doing theirs…"**

Your diagram will illuminate coworkers, activities, and data that staff might find valuable. Information they may not know exists suddenly becomes accessible. They might even identify data you could use to create new products or services or possibly sell to unserved markets to create new revenue streams.

Knowing how the organization works provides clarity and transparency to staff, management, customers, stakeholders, vendors, and everyone else the organization touches. It also provides the ability to adjust and fine-tune the work that gets done. Finally, it gives management the understanding of specific performance criteria that contribute to or inhibits success and the ability to objectively measure, correct, or reward behavior that creates it.

When change is rooted in the pursuit of best practices, it becomes easier to achieve. When a best practice change is driven by a group for the benefit of the group, the natural resistance to change is diminished. Even better, best practices identified by staff tend to be more effective, less costly, and easier to implement than when management imposes them.

The pursuit of best practices has two benefits: First, the seeds of disillusion planted by a spawning bureaucracy are quickly sterilized because the value of every person and the work they do is clear to everyone else in the organization. Second, it helps management and leadership identify efforts that are not supporting the overall customer experience and moving the organization toward its vision.

Perhaps the greatest benefit of a visual representation of your S&S is the clarity it brings to how each individual contributes to success, which is often a more effective motivator than money or praise. So it's time to start documenting your S&S.

*****

Logistics alone dictate that managing a growing number of employees and customers requires increasingly formal management systems. From duplication of work to failing to conform to legal guidelines, an ad hoc approach to getting things done simply doesn't scale.

A business cannot manage scheduling and vacations for one hundred and fifty employees the way it did when it had fifteen. A business cannot manage receivables, payables, and inventory or provide client support for three hundred customers the way it did when it had thirty.

Before a business grows into adulthood, most staff know one another and their responsibilities (G&R). As the business matures into adulthood, lack of control and clarity about responsibilities and authority can have devastating effects.

Bill's Anecdote
The Case of the $365,000 Check

The desk was old. The desk was small. The desk was designed to be as inefficient and ergonomically disruptive as possible. It wasn't in an office or even a room; it was in what could best be described as an unused hallway. The desk was to be my workplace. The desk and I were introduced by my contract manager, Bill.

"Here's where you'll be working."

"Thank you, Bill," after my desk and I first met.

What else could I say to the person who'd been forced to hire an outside consultant when he'd failed to move the project forward? The desk and its location clearly broadcast how the people I was going to be working with felt about my being there.

I began exploring my new workplace by opening and closing the sticky, ill-fitting drawers designed for use by a three-talon claw. The few minutes it took me to cycle through to "the drawer" felt like an hour.

It opened with a patient, self-aware dubiousness that exposed a check, silently waiting to be found after having been out of sight and out of mind for who knew how long.

I reached for the check and turned it over, looking for the issue date. All I could see were zeros, five of them with a three, six, five in front—$365,000.00—made out in loving laser printer ink with my client's name following "Pay to the Order Of." It took a moment to breathe and another to finally see the issue date. The check was four years and a few months old, sitting in an unused desk in a hallway.

Panic coursed through me as I dropped the check back into the drawer.

What am I supposed to do with this damn check?

Ignoring the fact that it had been sitting in this particular drawer silently waiting for years to be rediscovered, I was worried as the desk had no lock. I cautiously retrieved the check, hid it in my folio, rose, and went looking for Bill.

When I revealed what I'd found, Bill looked like I felt when I first saw the check. There were no words.

Together, we went looking for the right person to notify. A witch's brew of terror, hysteria, fear of reprisal, and incredulity followed us as we watched the information trickling up through the chain of command.

I should explain, the money was a drop in the bucket of this publicly traded insurance firm. Certainly not enough to change their reported income one hundredth of a percent. As the funds weren't part of an illegal enterprise, theft, or embezzlement, it was devilishly understandable that no one noticed the missing funds. Nonetheless, misplacing a check for hundreds of thousands of dollars doesn't happen every day. Surely an accounts receivable clerk or the customer would have noticed and said something.

While sleuthing out how a $365,000 check was left in the drawer of a decrepit old desk no one wanted to use, the important question was why nobody had noticed the funds were missing. Everyone Bill and I spoke to told us calmly, and without surprise, they had no knowledge of a missing $365,000 check. Incomprehensible. The reason was simple. The check had fallen through a crack in the company's complex accounting systems and not been canceled and reissued…because nobody noticed.

*****

On its face, the story seems unrealistic. How could such a thing ever happen, particularly with a public company and that much money? Granted, this took place in the late 1980s when computers were less prolific, supremely expensive, and difficult to implement. Systems and processes were unintentionally designed with hard-to-find gaps and holes before they mature into real problems. Adding to the lack of oversight, electronic error checking has been a problem looking for a solution since the first electronic computers were used.

Having bought my first business computer in 1973, my experience is, when a system allows mistakes, they are typically large and well hidden. Until you confront a big one, you're not going to worry about it. The cost of finding them (i.e., creating perfect technology systems) is rarely worth any harm that may arise. Understanding the ease with which these gaps and cracks become "built in" is difficult until you've fallen into one, like the $365,000 check I stumbled across.

This anecdote had a vastly different impact than other issues that often arise from weak or nonexistent systems and structure. Sending the wrong items to a customer with a critical, time-sensitive need can have ruinous results. Depending on the profile of your customer and your exposure in the market, other customers and prospects could quickly become fearful of consummating their first or next transaction with you.

~~Creating~~ Documenting Your Systems and Structure

The seventh Index indicator, S&S, is unique in that a business can be created and operate quite effectively without formalizing the other seven indicators. Unlike the other seven indicators, an organization without any systems or structure can't do basic operational activities such as inventory management, accounting, payroll, and many more. In short, you can't have a functioning organization without a few basic systems and some structure.

In that light, S&S can (and will) form organically, without forethought, preparation, or documentation, even when they are not proactively pursued. On the other hand, *operating quite effectively* is vastly different from having the ability to anticipate change and the resilience to prepare for and manage it. If a sustainable organization is your desire, all eight indicators are needed.

Because of their inescapable weed-like pervasiveness, the creation process for S&S becomes an effort to document what's already in place. Once completed, documentation evolves into refinement through implementation and maintenance. It can feel like reassembling a bin of shredded documents or putting together a five-thousand-piece jigsaw puzzle that's all the same color. As you begin the documentation process, it can be helpful to keep two tenets in mind:

- Most people want to do something meaningful, valuable, and financially rewarding; to do good and be good.
- When people understand how their organization works, they're more likely to grasp the impact of their efforts, adeptly refine processes, and improve organizational efficacy both collaboratively and independently.

I've found the best way to begin is with the same sponsors that helped create G&R. It's important to verify each person has proper authority to be privy to the information being gathered, which makes managers a preferred choice. There are two potential downsides to using managers.

First, they usually have limited capacity to add the additional commitment to their regular workload. Second, if what's written isn't clear to the most uninformed reader, there's a risk it will be misconstrued and create problems at some critical point of application. Much like instruction manuals or training curriculum, the writing skills needed for documenting S&S are specialized and not mandatory for most managers.

While I have no proven magic formula for finding the right people to execute this step, I recommend starting with a cross-functional team of individuals with excellent listening and written communication skills. Have them work with the individuals who are identifying, capturing, and documenting your S&S to mitigate and avoid the two common problems noted above.

Most organizations have three predominant process groups: sales, inventory management/fulfillment, and human resources. The easiest starting point tends to be the sales processes.

Begin with activities that find and attract customers. From that point, imagine you're following a map and document every activity from closing a sale to processing payment.

As products are sold, they're usually restocked or replaced. Follow that trail and document inventory management activities. Each step along these two paths often has several subordinate activities that need to be identified and captured. Special order handling, warranty and repair services, and labor and customer support are three examples. Like any good explorer, make sure you pursue and document every recurring offshoot from the main path.

The third predominant group is personnel-related activities: recruitment, hiring, management, development, promotion, and a host of other operational, regulatory, and legal human resource requirements every business must comply with. At the mature stage of development, most firms have employee manuals that can serve as excellent starting points for S&S documentation.

There are often people-related S&S that aren't fully addressed in an employee manual due to legal requirements and constraints, such as recruitment practices and how key performance indicators (KPI) are defined. If certain positions have minimum educational or physical requirements, asking how they impact the responsibilities of a position can help identify esoteric S&S.

Almost every organization has a fourth thread of proprietary cyclic activities whose inclusion or exclusion can have substantial impact. Examples include accounting, maintenance, security, disaster recovery, certifications for people and equipment, perishables, obsolescence, information technology upgrades, training, and many more.

When sponsors have completed capturing your S&S, they must be put into an easily shared and understandable format. The ERD and DFD described in the Index indicator no. 7, "Systems and Structure" section above are two potential starting points. I highly recommend recruiting someone from your sales or marketing staff to design something with a creative, proprietary flair that will make its documentation more fun, interesting, and consumable.

Once the first draft has been completed, each department, division, or distinct area of your organization must review and verify each segment relevant to their areas of responsibility. After the second draft, the entire model needs to be shared with all staff. These processes have five objectives:

1. Verify alignment with management's intentions.[60]
2. Confirm documentation is clearly understood.
3. Identify superfluous activities.
4. Expose duplication of effort.
5. Schedule regular review and revision of policies and procedures.

---

[60] This can be an ideal opportunity for staff to share new ideas and management to learn from the experience and knowledge of those most connected to the work being done.

Note: Having documented and implemented G&R increases the value and benefits of documented S&S.

Implementing Your Systems and Structure

Unlike G&R, S&S are already in place, whether documented or not, and implementation involves a modified approach. For value to be realized and a return on investment of time and costs to be reaped, staff must be given access to these operational details and made aware of their existence.

An S&S diagram is an uncommon mapping tool to most people; therefore, its use and value often need to be proactively taught. Internalizing routine activities depicted with a map can be counter-intuitive. Additionally, most people know their job, and understanding the bigger picture doesn't automatically seem valuable.

As described in chapter 2, decreased flexibility creates predictable issues, including

- staff routinely bumping into barriers that limit their ability to do their job,
- policies and procedures taking precedence over serving the customer,
- client requests becoming harder to accommodate, and
- staff forced to say "no" or "I can't do that" more frequently.

When individuals cut corners or ignore the building blocks of S&S such as policies, procedures, and the chain of command, others will feel licensed to ignore them when it suits them. When that happens, success created by a talented staff doing good work often leads to a work environment that is toxic to many of those who helped create it.

Therefore, creating respect and adherence to S&S is often an exercise in reminding everyone of the benefits:

- A better understanding of how everyone's efforts are connected to the organization's purpose (connection to purpose)

- A better understanding of how everyone's efforts are connected to the individuals and organizations they serve (connection to customer)
- A better understanding of how everyone's efforts are connected to each other (teamwork and collaboration)
- Identifying opportunities to collaboratively learn, grow, and continuously find better ways to do things (best practices)

Achieving these benefits depends on everyone's embrace of collaboration, a desire to pursue the organization's vision, and sharing a common commitment to the interdependence described in chapter 9. The results of a successful S&S implementation are increased staff engagement and organizational efficacy.

Maintaining Your Systems and Structure

There are two common drivers of change to your S&S, some of the most stable aspects of operations. One is external change to the environment you operate in or the community you serve. The other is self-imposed change. Maintaining your S&S requires integrating these two. The process of doing so is most easily achieved by starting with their impact in terms of degrees of separation.

One degree of separation would be a change that has a direct or immediate impact on an individual, activity, or process. If the impact is felt anywhere beyond that initial point of effect, it would be considered two degrees of separation. Each subsequent down-the-line impact represents an increasing degree.

Documenting the impacts and degrees of separation allows you to quantify the costs and benefits of making almost any change and objectively evaluate whether to move forward or not. If the decision to proceed is made, you have a blueprint of all the S&S that need to be revised or updated to accommodate the changes.

As you can see, change tends to disrupt the normal flow of business and create friction. That friction can occur both quickly and over time, in different ways with different aspects of interaction for all stakeholders—even when the net result is positive.

As a business grows, change becomes more difficult. It requires increased consumption of the three critical, finite, nonrenewable resources: people, time, and money. Increased complexity makes it harder to identify areas where a small change may have a large impact in another area of the organization. Because of complex interconnectivity of the parts and pieces, changing any one of them can have unintended consequences.

I wanted to know if there was a way we could plan and manage these unexpected results of our system development efforts. "Unintended Consequences" are basically unwanted emergent properties. And just like the senseless task of looking for an "unknown, unknown" risk, how can you predict the unpredictable? [61]

When pressure to adopt systemic or structural change triggers a perceived need for operational change, the first activity should be to review the S&S.

Reflecting on Systems and Structure

This chapter describes a new and different way to think about systems and structure for most leaders. To survive, businesses need to reinforce their abilities to thrive and grow. Whether your business needs to create, implement, or maintain systems and structure, the following questions will help reveal their potential and identify clever ways to apply and capitalize on this vital tool.

- How do you know if tasks or activities are being duplicated?
- How do you know when codependent departments are out of step with one another?
- What are a few creative ways you can improve connectivity to purpose and customers with documented systems and structure? What about teamwork? What about best practices and collaboration or any of the other benefits mentioned in this chapter?

---

[61] SE Scholar, Emergence: The Mystery of Systems Engineering, October 3 2010. http://se-scholar.com/se-blog/2010/10/emergence-mystery-of-systems.html.

- Does your organization *have* systems and structure?
- Are they documented, not in someone's head?
- Are they understood, embraced, and modeled by leadership and staff?
- How do you know?

Accessing and completing the Index scorecard survey is explained in chapter 12.

Key Points

Ch 1	Operational Imperatives	Clarity of purpose	Consistency of performance	Engagement of people
Ch 2	Stage of Maturity	Youth	Adolescence	Adulthood
Ch 2	Why leaders fail to achieve the 3 Ps	They didn't know they needed to do them.	They didn't know how to do them.	They forgot they needed to do them.
Ch 3	Arc of Success	New Ideas ► Growth ► Complexity ► Controls ► Less Flexibility		
Ch 3	Problems with Success	Symptoms masquerading as root problems	Historically good operational behaviors that begin to create undesirable results	Emotional resistance to beneficial change
Ch 3	Index Indicators & (chapter #)	Values (4) Vision (5) Mission (6)	Business Plan (7) Marketing Plans (8) Goals and Responsibilities (9)	**Systems and Structure (10)** Communications Plan

Tenets to keep in mind when capturing S&S:

1. People want to do something meaningful, valuable, and personally fruitful—to do good and to be good.
2. If people understand how the organization works, they can grasp the impact of their efforts, aka contributions, and can collaboratively and independently refine processes and improve results.

As businesses grow, the distance between customer, staff, and operations that create products and deliver services also grows. Systems and structure are critical for creating engagement among staff, and ensuring the needs of the customer will be served.

G&R is a failure point for adolescent organizations because they cannot mature into adulthood without them. S&S is the first inevitable failure point for mature organizations.

While G&R outlined in chapter 9 and S&S are inherently connected, they are not codependent. Most organizations have three predominant process groups, sales, inventory management, and human resources. The easiest starting point tends to be the sales processes.

The burden of capturing all your S&S is far outweighed by the benefits.

Four primary benefits of systems and structure:

*   Connection to purpose
*   Connection to customers
*   Teamwork and collaboration
*   Best practices

CHAPTER 11

Information Sharing: Communications Plan

Index Indicator No. 8

Developing engagement, the third and final operational imperative, faces the last two mountains to be scaled before reaching profitable sustainability. The first, providing a sense of purpose coupled with some degree of control is enabled by S&S. The second, the ability to access and share information with ease and confidence that can be enabled with a communications plan.

The larger an organization becomes, the greater the difficulty in achieving timely, accurate, and dependable communication both internally and externally. In concert with this frictional necessity, one of the valuable benefits of growth is the ease of increasing diversity.

Whether physically healthy, disabled, or suffering from cultural disparities, *staff must be able to communicate effectively regardless of their role.* The inability to do so creates problems that lead to adverse results. Given five senses to work with, communication arguably offers the broadest spectra of effective tools and styles. Therefore, creating organizational standards and objective measures of proficiency are ambitious and challenging.

Minimizing communication risks and maximizing benefits are skills that can be developed and should become routine for every organization. The most effective tool I've found for doing so is a communications plan.

Benefits

Creating, documenting, and implementing a communications plan has six benefits: culture of communication, connection to purpose, connection to…everything else that matters, preparedness, conduits and connectors, and onboarding.

Culture of communication

People are usually more comfortable with clear guidelines for what information needs to be shared with whom, when, and how. Knowing they have a place to get those details when needed is calming and reduces anxiety. Emergencies are less disruptive, emotions don't escalate as quickly or often, resolutions and decisions tend to be better and made sooner.

Having clarity about information that needs to be distributed, knowing where to find it quickly, without disruption, and distribute it provides an emotional comfort level similar to being embraced by a warm security blanket.

Connection to purpose

Purpose in the Index model encompasses vision, mission, and values.[62] If the need for growth in the number of staff has been minimized through the organization's maturation process, it becomes inescapable in adulthood. Maintaining a pervasive connection to purpose by staff is more difficult as staff size grows.

Over time, staff growth also increases the degree of separation between leadership and the customer, making it harder for leadership to have direct, accurate insight into the changes their customers are dealing with. Those changes are the very things that can make a mission statement obsolete and undermine the ability to deliver value or retain customers. A workforce with a robust communications plan

---

[62] As defined in chapters 4–7.

is one of the best ways to avoid these problems while bridging the growing gaps between customers, staff, and leadership.

Connecting to…everything else that matters

The ability to communicate in a manner most likely to ensure recipients fully and accurately understand the message minimizes wasted time and effort. It increases engagement and minimizes the negative impacts of change. Unless you communicate with people in ways they're familiar and comfortable with, you lose credibility.

Using a communications plan ensures staff knows whom they're connected to in pursuit of their vision and fulfilling their mission. It gives them clarity about whom to talk to if they have any uncertainty or disagreements. Two advantages of engagement are receptivity to new ideas and ability to gain support. Knowledge, insight, and awareness are all improved when people connect with one another.

Preparedness

Simply being connected is not enough. Efficient distribution and use of data are also required to ensure it's reaching those who need it and have the ability to use it for benefit.

A communications plan takes the guesswork out of wondering whom to notify when something unexpected happens or sudden needs arise. It helps ensure the right people are notified in a well-timed manner with relevant details in the way best suited to each recipient. Using a formalized plan also minimizes potentially adverse results that can come from unanticipated delays or failure to notify the people expecting a particular outcome of changes.

Conduits and connectors; the people

Conduits are the natural conveyors of information. They often have a reputation for knowing what's happening and passing it on, and they're well-known. They grease the wheels of information distribution. When news travels through the company unofficially, conduits are responsible.

Connectors are the social navigators within your organization. They have the answers to questions or know how to get them. Connectors know whom to go to when there's a decision to be made, a need fulfilled, or information located.

The ability to identify these key individuals reduces the time required to effectively communicate and provides insight to leadership as to the often-overlooked value they bring to most operational activities.

Lack of resources is a common complaint when the idea of developing a communications plan is discussed. One of the best justifications for prioritizing the effort is the identification of conduits and connectors within your organization.

Onboarding

People are the single most expensive asset of most businesses. Whether adding new staff, replacing someone lost to retirement, or being a poor fit, a communications plan coupled with documented systems and structure make the task of onboarding immensely easier, faster, and more effective. In this context, onboarding applies to more than just new hires. It can also be valuable in helping existing staff transition to a new role, department, job, even location.

The ability to quickly and accurately onboard new staff should be a prerequisite for the human resources department of every growing firm. Employee manuals should address it, yet all too often it remains an afterthought or missing. The investment of time, money, and people in the development and deployment of a communications plan tends to pay dividends from the moment the effort begins and rarely diminishes.

Jennifer's Anecdote
Help, I Need a Favor

Working in a high-stress environment means familiarity with unexpected problems and the pressure to react quickly. When Jennifer, my counterpart and one of the firm's seasoned legal secretaries came to me in confidence, I could tell by the look on her face this was going to be one of those moments.

"We have a problem."

Her statement confirmed my assumption.

In a large law firm like ours, it's not uncommon for executive assistants from multiple practice areas to work on separate elements of a transaction for a client. Who's doing what for whom isn't always clear, which requires the lead assistant to stay on top of all the research, work product, and communications with the client.

When so many different activities are connected by a common client, what happens in one area can easily and quickly impact other areas and individuals. This was one of those situations.

Jennifer's tone and demeanor encompassed the unspoken details:

- The problem was with an important client.
- It had to involve more than one person in the firm.
- There was a lot of risk and money at stake.
- She came to me, not one of several other of our attorneys working on the transaction.
- The worst? Jennifer didn't know what to do, which made us both anxious.

When problems find their way to me, my preferred approach is to begin by hearing from everyone involved to get a complete picture of what happened and their perspective of the problem. In this case, getting this information was relatively simple: Jennifer had all I needed to hear.

We were working on a complex real estate transaction, and the client had two problems. They had contract deadlines that had to be met coupled with regulatory county, state, and federal criteria that also had to be met. The contract deadlines did not allow enough time to achieve the regulatory timelines. There was no wiggle room.

Maryanne, the executive assistant for this client, called Jennifer, the secretary for one of our practice-area lawyers. Maryanne wanted Jennifer to fabricate a document and not tell any of the lawyers. Her argument was that if nobody complained, by the time it would come to light, everything would be over and done. No harm, no foul.

After the way she had been pressured by the client to create the document, Jennifer was emotionally unprepared to tell the client no and be responsible for losing them. She certainly wasn't willing to tell one of the attorneys she worked for and risk being blamed for putting the client's contract with our firm in jeopardy.

Surely, in time, I, too, would find myself in Jennifer's position. Management's guidance or direction for such a situation was not documented and had never been discussed. Suddenly who to ask and who to tell became my number one concern for my upcoming review.

*****

Creating Your Communications Plan

The single biggest problem in communication is the illusion that it has taken place.

—George Bernard Shaw[63]

Communication is one of those things most of us do every day. Creating a plan for doing something so ubiquitous doesn't always seem like the best investment of time. If you've arrived at this chapter eager to get started, you're in the minority. Most don't want to go to the trouble.

---

[63] Shaw, George Bernard. "George Bernard Shaw > Quotes > Quotable Quote," *Goodreads*. Goodreads Inc. https://www.goodreads.com/quotes/178425-the-single-biggest-problem-in-communication-is-the-illusion-that.

Creating tools that improve communication becomes easier when guided by the desire to stay in business. Neither negative predispositions nor biases diminish their importance. Investing in creating a communications plan is one example of working on your business, not in it, and produces unexpectedly positive ROIs. The need and value are so great a communications plan should be one of the highest priorities for every mature business.

There are three universal goals for a communications plan:

1. Provide information that improves decision-making, meaningful feedback, and strategic planning. This calls for anticipation of reactions or implications of events or decisions for various internal and external stakeholders. Realizing this goal usually requires routine, consistent messaging.
2. Create support and buy-in for activities and decisions when individuals may not be fully aware of their importance or understand the risks of not doing so. Successful achievement of this goal is usually increased when proven change-management practices are embedded in creation and implementation efforts. While this goal is always relevant internally, it commonly applies to external communications with vendors and customers.
3. Make sure everyone's on the same page when unexpected changes occur.

Begin by assembling representatives from all areas of your organization to document the priorities and interests of your stakeholders. Group the findings by similarities (e.g., responsibilities, interests, routines, etc.). Don't forget to consider outside sources.[64]

---

[64] Including external stakeholders such as vendors, customers, and professional service providers in your plan is tricky. The guidelines for communication with these people are often proprietary and handled by specific internal staff based on assigned responsibilities. Including or excluding them in your plan is dependent on several specific contextual and situational aspects, which is beyond the scope of this book.

Two additional factors to consider when grouping are levels of authority and responsibility. Sometimes information needs to be controlled while decisions are still being made. Along with making sausage and laws, decision-making is not always for the faint of heart and should be done by a select group of individuals with good reason for involvement.

Your groupings will help define proprietary communication details and minimize emotional obstacles such as resistance to change and the need to compromise. When defining your groups, review your systems and structure to help identify the conduits and connectors. Every group should have at least one of each.

Attempting to document every possible problem or need that may arise is a fool's errand. The attributes defined in the plan for each group must explain the need for regular updates along with the frequency and manner of distribution. Some examples of groupings I've seen include

- sales and marketing staff,
- administrative staff,
- project participants,
- midlevel management, and
- specific product and/or service consumers.

Grouping for communications purposes is a highly proprietary exercise. Ensuring alignment with authority and responsibility among group members must be considered as your plan is developed. Every group you create should pass the purpose litmus test, i.e, activities and efforts should support delivering on your mission and move the business closer to your vision while guided by your values.

One of the more complex aspects of developing a communications plan is balancing consistency and manageability with retaining flexibility to accommodate differences between various areas, sections, departments, or divisions common to most mature organizations.

When organizations reach adulthood, various work groups routinely need to develop their own ways of doing things that differ from company norms. This lack of consistency creates potential for conflict around freedom to independently develop tools, processes, and procedures in their work group. The risk of conflict grows when people interact with other work groups where variations exist. The potential for "The grass is greener elsewhere" can become a lure.

Pursuit of a shared vision while working to deliver on a shared mission should be the thread that pulls people together when internal differences arise.

The ideal situation is an organic distribution of best (communication) practices everyone can embrace while doing what works best for them. Clear guidelines for what managers and staff need to know must be documented. The manner data is gathered can vary dramatically. How that data is distributed requires some organizational consistency.

Implementing Your Communications Plan

Much like the department of redundancy department, implementing a communications plan is in itself an exercise in effective communication. It is essential that the plan be easy to find and access, well organized, intuitive, and understandable. Validating these attributes requires some testing and evaluation on a cross section of individuals and departments.

Once validated, the plan should provide insight into how to communicate it with the rest of your company. After all, this is simply another message that needs to be shared and understood by all staff.

Managers and supervisors need to be trained and ready. Everyone will need opportunities to practice. Undoubtedly, the ability to realize value from a new tool depends on the amount of change required to use it. As email is a central element of communication for most organizations, email writing and distribution guidelines are often an excellent way to begin.

Leadership in each area of your company should be able to point to relevant examples of routine communication that could be improved using the guidelines in your new plan. After all, much of the plan should have come from them or their colleagues. They should share those benefits with direct reports and encourage their use.

The process tends to gain credibility with the understanding that speaking and listening are two of three components of good communication. Ensuring a message is delivered and received as intended requires observation. Without observation, 33 percent of our communication skills are being ignored.

Three sayings I've heard since childhood:

- Do as I say, not as I do.
- Actions speak louder than words.
- Don't judge people by what they say; judge them by what they do.

Each supports the notion that the ability to see how people act or react to various forms of messaging can have a drastic impact on comprehension. The way information is delivered becomes key to getting the right message across and avoiding people hearing or reading what they want.

Instilling belief in the equal importance of each component of communication becomes the foundation on which transcendent communication is built. It is one of the limited yet powerful ways you and your staff can help your organization stand above the crowd.

The last thing to consider and review is the degree of formality in your plan, which should be guided and evaluated by risk. The more critical the need or complex the issue, the more formality is needed to ensure success. When formality is excessive, the seeds of bureaucracy are sown. A friend and colleague once commented, "A culture of communication can forestall the need for bureaucratic structure." Avoiding this trap requires conveying the critical nature of the need for using this tool to your staff.

Maintaining Your Communications Plan

Almost everything that happens in or around your business, whether internal or external, can affect the suitability of your communications plan. Maintenance requires vigilant monitoring and responsive training or plan modification when results do not meet expectations.

Occasionally, triggers unrelated to individual performance or adherence to guidelines can occur. Common examples include changes in organizational structure, responsibilities, markets being served, products and services being offered, and other variations on existing business activities.

These changes can create a disconnect between sender and recipient. In these circumstances, details guiding the distribution of information can quickly become ineffective or obsolete and require updates.

Reflecting on Your Communications Plan

This chapter describes a new and different way to think about a communications plan for most leaders. To survive, businesses need to reinforce their abilities to thrive and grow. Whether your business needs to create, implement, or maintain a communications plan, the following questions will help reveal their potential and identify clever ways to apply and capitalize on this vital tool:

- How does your staff find answers to questions or communicate concerns regarding business, client, vendor, or personal matters?
- How do you ensure safe and timely distribution of confidential or time-sensitive information?
- How does your business facilitate and promote regular interaction among staff, managers, supervisors, and/or departments?
- What are a few creative ways you can create a culture of communication using a communications plan? What about utilizing conduits and connectors? What about preparedness or any of the other benefits mentioned in this chapter?
- Does your organization *have* a communications plan?
- Is it documented, not in someone's head?

- Is it understood, embraced, and utilized by leadership and staff?
- How do you know?

Accessing and completing the Index scorecard survey is explained in chapter 12.

Key Points

Ch 1	Operational Imperatives	Clarity of purpose	Consistency of performance	Engagement of people
Ch 2	Stage of Maturity	Youth	Adolescence	Adulthood
Ch 2	Why leaders fail to achieve the 3 Ps	They didn't know they needed to do them.	They didn't know how to do them.	They forgot they needed to do them.
Ch 3	Arc of Success	New Ideas ► Growth ► Complexity ►Controls ► Less Flexibility		
Ch 3	Problems with Success	Symptoms masquerading as root problems	Historically good operational behaviors that begin to create undesirable results	Emotional resistance to beneficial change
Ch 3	Index Indicators & (chapter #)	Values (4) Vision (5) Mission (6)	Business Plan (7) Marketing Plans (8) Goals and Responsibilities (9)	Systems and Structure (10) **Communications Plan (11)**

Organizations in adulthood have complexities that bring benefits and risks. One of the major benefits is the ability to easily increase diversity and leverage the differences among people.

Significant increases in the number and overhead of rules and regulations create greater risk and liability.

The need and value of an internal communications plan are so great having one should be one of the highest priorities for every mature business.

There are three components of communication:

- Speaking
- Listening
- Observing

A good communications plan fulfills three objectives:

- Improve decision-making.
- Create support and buy-in for changer efforts.
- Ensure alignment throughout the organization.

Implementing a communications plan is an exercise in effectively communicating.

The degree of formality in a communications plan depends on risk. The greater the risks, the greater the need for formality.

When formality is excessive, the seeds of bureaucracy are sown.

Six primary benefits of a communications plan are as follows:

- Culture of communication
- Connection to purpose
- Connecting to…everything else that matters
- Preparedness
- Conduits and connectors
- Onboarding

PART 5

CRYSTALLIZATION

You are not here merely to make a living. You are here in order to enable the world to live more amply, with greater vision, with a finer spirit of hope and achievement. You are here to enrich the world, and you impoverish yourself if you forget the errand.

—Woodrow Wilson[65]

When a group of individuals comes together for a common purpose, it's typically called a business or an organization. Whether a not- for-profit venture, government agency, or for-profit enterprise, the

[65] Wilson, Woodrow. "Woodrow T. Wilson Quotes," *QuoteHD*. QuoteHD. http://www.quotehd.com/quotes/woodrow-t-wilson-quote-you-are-not-here-merely-to-make-a-living-you-ar.

human element is the backbone. This element will always result in one of three possible truths:

1. They're going to commit suicide through a combination of bad management and poor decision-making.
2. They're doomed to failure because their efforts are based on assumptions and perceptions, not facts and reality.
3. Their organization will thrive and prosper now and long after they are gone.

Conclusion?

Contrary to popular excuses, businesses don't fail. Failure isn't due to an invasion of external factors. When a business fails, it's a DIY (do-it-yourself) effort.

My research exposed the most consistently effective way to avoid business suicide. Focus on achieving three operational imperatives: clarity of purpose, consistency of performance, and engagement of people. All you need to do now is identify the weakest indicators in your business and start strengthening them one by one.

CHAPTER 12

On Becoming an Outstanding Organization

*Confidence is going after Moby Dick in a rowboat
and taking tartar sauce with you.*

—Zig Ziglar[66]

Deep within your business lay the seeds of its own destruction. Unseen and unnoticed, they can cause strange things:

- Leadership, sales, and IT act as if they're serving three different masters.
- You have identified high-value customers and can't get them to notice you.
- You have smart people, and thoughtless mistakes keep happening.

Do any of these sound familiar?
"We're not sure where this company is going."
"We're not sure who our potential market is."
"We're not sure how we add value to this company."

---

[66] Ziglar, Zig. *Quote Master.* https://www.quotemaster.org/qb536d37b7d569 195e321ab128658e90d.

It would be insane to kill your business for no reason, but you might be—not from anything you've done, but from something you haven't.

I see profitable, growing businesses as candidates for becoming exceptional. Outstanding organizations that want to be successful and thought of as extraordinary places to work, with devoted customers and dedicated employees, people who think about the business like you do. Then reality sets in. Awareness soon follows; how complex and time-consuming these desires can become.

Leaders want to be active contributors to the success of their organizations. This motivation is what pulls them into the future. The degree to which they can simultaneously focus on the future and the present depends a great deal on how well their organizations are performing.

> *"...an ever-present conflict exists between two areas of focus: the mundane of the here and now and the exhilaration of successes yet to come."*

Aware that most leaders have precious little time to think, much less the luxury of looking ahead, an ever-present conflict exists between two areas of focus: the mundane of the here and now and the exhilaration of successes yet to come.

Getting Started: Start small, be focused and deliberate

The effort to create and incorporate all eight Index indicators into your organization can feel overwhelming. Don't try to do it all at once. Using the Index scorecard, evaluate each indicator for your organization and focus on the weakest ones first. Successful implementation of these indicators can and will reveal unexplored opportunities for efficiencies and immediate relief of time and financial pressures.

When leaders find ways to make these efforts less disruptive to the creative aspects of leadership, they can focus on the future, the big picture, the vision they had when they first began. The familiar saying "It's not about the destination, it's about the journey" is true. It's on the journey we learn the valuable lessons of how to reach the destination.

Consider assembling staff from throughout your organization in a large room filled with flip charts, asking each person to list their wants and concerns and to include examples from the past, present, and future.

This collaborative exercise would produce pages of issues your organization was, is, and likely will be dealing with. Envision pointing to any one issue from anywhere in the room and asking the group, "If we were able to fix this issue, what other issues (that are actually nothing more than symptoms) would we be able to take off our lists? Which wants would we be able to make happen?"

As you worked through the lists removing items, you and your staff would have identified the real issues, set the attention-seeking symptoms aside, and exposed the deepest problems and desires without being distracted. That kind of clarity creates focus and energy that leads to results.

This effective yet time-consuming process is streamlined with the Index scorecard.

"the index scorecard survey can be found at https://businessesdontfail.com/fsc800723/"

The Index is noteworthy for is its ability to objectively measure an organization's weaknesses with a practical, "easy-to-use, easy-to-understand scorecard." Its significance is its keen accuracy with minimal investments of time. Its value is in its ability to objectively measure subjective organizational characteristics: clarity of purpose, consistency of performance, and engagement of people. Completing the

Index scorecard survey generates a psychological commitment from the implicit need to face the underlying truth of *each individual's personal reality*.

My Business *Managers* Reality Index is intended for management. Having nonmanagerial staff complete an Index scorecard survey can be valuable for assessing large, self-directed, or independent departments. *Caution*: doing so can be problematic for nonmanagement staff due to their limited knowledge of related goings-on outside their departments.

The Index scorecard survey can be found at https://businessesdontfail. com/fsc800723/

After using this effective tool, you'll have a list of Index indicators ranked by relative strength from your weakest to strongest. Efforts to strengthen your business and develop profitable sustainability should always *begin with one of your three weakest indicators*.

The unique circumstances of each business must be considered when determining the first indicator to work on. Investing in immediate needs versus long-term goals is always a balancing act. Be careful to avoid allowing a false sense of urgency to undermine the very real need to plan and prepare. While the use of time and money for things that may not appear to have immediate value can be characterized as unproductive, focusing on one of the three weakest indicators will reduce distractions and produce immediate relief of time and financial pressures.

Facing change while developing new skills

Developing the skills to create, implement, and maintain each indicator is a hallmark of good leadership. When new skills are required to address new needs and unfamiliar issues, their pursuit often creates friction. Friction that causes leaders to dismiss change and avoid developing those new skills.

It's too easy to double down on what worked in the past. This behavioral characteristic is further explored in a Harvard Business

Review article titled "Why Leaders Don't Embrace the Skills They'll Need for the Future."[67]

> The primary challenge most large companies now face is disruption, which requires a new strategy, new processes, and a new set of behaviors. But if employees have long been valued and rewarded for (specific) behaviors, why wouldn't they find it uncomfortable to suddenly embrace (different) behaviors? When we feel uncomfortable or stressed, we tend to double down on what has worked for us before.

Pursuit of the eight Index indicator components is not a contest or a series of milestones. No one individual can implement all of them, nor should they. Certainly not the boss. Each indicator stimulates specific benefits and mitigates specific issues common to varying stages of maturity. I recommend focusing on the benefits.

As you work through this process, your scorecard results will change. The disruptive problems demanding attention will decrease. Your business will begin performing more smoothly and profitably. Eventually, the 3Ps will become the foundation of your business.

For any of these indicators to be meaningful in your company, they need to be actively used. Over time, each component will continue to provide a means to developing better understanding between leadership and staff, working together uncovering hidden potential. It's about a team working collaboratively, building trust and camaraderie. Remember, it's the journey.

Creating an outstanding organization, aka a profitable, growing, sustainable enterprise, doesn't happen just because a business has excellent employees or great products and services to offer. It takes

---

[67] Schwarts, Tony and Emily Pines. "Why Leaders Don't Embrace the Skills They'll Need for the Future." Harvard Business Review. October 25, 2018.

foresight and planning, risks and assumptions, trial and error, good decisions and bad ones. Most of all, it takes persistence because, as my dad used to say, *"you can't fail if you never stop trying."*

INDEX

ABOUT THE AUTHOR

A nonrecovering serial entrepreneur, Larry Mandelberg solves complex business problems. With a four-generation head start, this consultant, speaker, and author represents the fifth generation of his family's business, inheriting "170 years of successful organizational experience."

Larry is an effective catalyst for change who achieved new levels of success and growth for businesses in industries as diverse as software, automotive aftermarket, education, and agriculture.

Propelled into writing from his years of experience, Larry has published more than eighty columns ("Eyes on Business") and developed a loyal following. His first book, *Businesses Don't Fail, They Commit Suicide*, details his decades-long search for the answer to "Why do businesses fail?" and his findings.

Mandelberg is a student of organizational lifecycles and has developed the Business Managers Reality Index to help businesses create sustainable growth and avoid business suicide. The Index is noteworthy for its ability to objectively measure an organization's weaknesses with a practical, easy-to-use, easy-to-understand scorecard. Its significance is its keen accuracy with minimal investments of time. Its value is in its ability to objectively measure subjective organizational characteristics: clarity of purpose, consistency of performance, and engagement of people. The Index scorecard induces a psychological commitment from the implicit need to face the underlying truth of each individual's personal reality.

Larry has launched four start-ups, led a merger, and conducted a successful turnaround. Among his thirteen businesses, he's also had the unfortunate pleasure of suffering business suicide firsthand.

Mr. Mandelberg has been a guest on television and radio programs talking about business and entrepreneurship. He provides leadership team development, change mentoring, strategic planning, executive coaching, and ethics training to midsize organizations and their boards through his consulting practice.

Larry has been delightfully married to his wife, Nancy, since 1982. He received his MBA from Drexel University and currently serves as board chairman for Innovative Education Management. Mandelberg has provided training for Cooperative Personnel Services (Influence with Integrity) and taught team-building classes for the Sacramento Entrepreneurship Academy.

Larry may be reached at https://mandelberg.biz/.

www.ingramcontent.com/pod-product-compliance
Lightning Source LLC
Chambersburg PA
CBHW071246150726
48001CB00018B/195